OSWALD JACOBY, who introduces this book, is the most famous all-round player of games combining skill and chance in the world, and an author of leading works on poker, gin rummy, canasta, bridge, and backgammon. In the relatively short history of international backgammon competition, he has won four out of seven world championships.

His wife, MARY ZITA JACOBY, is a backgammon player and teacher of the top rank. She has taught backgammon for over ten years, given lectures on backgammon throughout the country, and established herself as the world's leading woman backgammon player by winning the first consolation event in two major backgammon tournaments and twice being a semi-finalist.

Their son, JAMES JACOBY, is well known for his bridge exploits, including three world championships, in addition to such bestselling books as *Instant Bridge.* He now devotes increasing time to backgammon and has won numerous tournaments, including the 1970 consolation event at the World Championship of Backgammon in Las Vegas.

The New York Times
BOOK OF BACKGAMMON

by
JAMES OSWALD
and
MARY ZITA JACOBY

Introduction by Oswald Jacoby

A PLUME BOOK
NEW AMERICAN LIBRARY
TIMES MIRROR
NEW YORK AND SCARBOROUGH, ONTARIO

PLUME TRADEMARK REG. PAT. OFF. AND FOREIGN COUNTRIES
REGISTERED TRADEMARK—MARCA REGISTRADA
HECHO EN FORGE VILLAGE, MASS., U.S.A.

SIGNET, SIGNET CLASSICS, MENTOR, PLUME and
MERIDIAN BOOKS are published *in the United States* by
The New American Library, Inc.,
1301 Avenue of the Americas, New York, New York 10019,
in Canada by The New American Library of Canada Limited,
81 Mack Avenue, Scarborough, Ontario M1L 1M8.

First Plume Printing, October, 1974

5   6   7   8   9   10   11   12   13

Printed in The United States of America

CONTENTS

FOREWORD

Mary Zita Jacoby may or may not be the best woman backgammon player in the world but she certainly is the best teacher —male or female.

James Oswald Jacoby is principally known as a bridge player. He is the only man under forty to ever acquire over 10,000 master points and, in addition, has managed to pick up three world championships.

In spite of this, backgammon is his favorite game. He has done well in the few tournaments he has had a chance to play in, and in my slightly prejudiced opinion is now as good at the game as anybody, anywhere.

In the last year Mary Zita has been teaching backgammon class after backgammon class. She needed lessons to do this teaching and Jim and I helped her prepare a set.

It occurred to me that there was material in these lessons for a book. I wanted to write it but my wife and son put their feet down and said that I had done enough writing.

Then they went ahead and produced this book—a series of lessons that will enable beginners to learn the game quickly, that will help good players become experts, and even give the greatest experts a chance to add to their knowledge of the game!

I am proud of them and believe firmly that they have written the best backgammon book of all time.

Oswald Jacoby
Dallas, Texas

PREFACE

This book is designed not only to enable the beginner to become a good backgammon player, but also to enable the good backgammon player to become an excellent player. It is presented in the form of twelve lessons.

While written with the beginner in mind, every lesson has points that good players will do well to pick up if they wish to improve their game. As for the top backgammon experts, they won't agree with everything in this book but we expect they all will read it —if only to see how we disagree with them. Of course, they also disagree with each other; you can't be an expert at anything and not have definite opinions.

In our search for ways to simplify the game for the average player we have formulated some rules that even the greatest experts will do well to learn. The most important of these concerns the Doubling Number, an invention which is described in the lesson on doubles and redoubles. Next is the rule for positioning one's last men. The opening moves recommended here represent the opinion of many of our top players but, as you would expect, not all.

We wish to express our sincere thanks to: Captain William H. Benson, U.S.N. (Ret.), who worked extensively with us on the entire book; Prince Alexis Obolensky, who is largely responsible for popularizing the game; the other backgammon experts whose brains we have picked; and, finally, Oswald Jacoby—the current backgammon champion of the world—who also happens to be our father and husband, respectively.

James Oswald Jacoby
Richardson, Texas

Mary Zita Jacoby
Dallas, Texas

August, 1973

The New York Times

BOOK OF
BACKGAMMON

Lesson I

SO YOU WANT TO PLAY BACKGAMMON

Learning a game is similar to learning a language. You not only must extend your vocabulary by adding new words and their meanings, but also must learn how to organize the new words into coherent and useful patterns. Even if you have played backgammon previously we urge you not to skip any of this lesson. It is quite likely that you are unfamiliar with some of the fine—but therefore the more important—points discussed.

To start at the beginning—backgammon is basically a two-handed game. It is suggested, however, that you obtain a back-gammon set and play against yourself as you go through these lessons. There is no question that following this suggestion will result in improving your understanding of the game. You will need certain equipment to play the game: a backgammon board, thirty men (fifteen of one color and fifteen of another color), and a pair of dice. A second pair of dice, two dice cups, and a doubling cube come with most sets. You should always use the dice cups. They frequently are designed with a narrow ridge on the inner side of the lip which acts to toss the dice about as they are thrown and to insure, as far as possible, an honest roll of the dice. The beginner has no need for the doubling cube. Its use will be discussed in Lesson VI.

The board is designed with twenty-four triangular playing positions which are colored alternately. These playing positions,

called "points," are divided by a blank space extending across
the board into two groups of twelve points each. We have numbered the different points as shown in Diagram I-1. Further, we

Diagram I-1

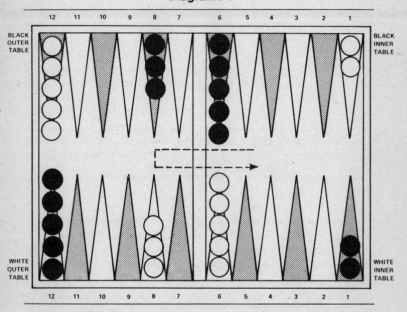

have selected white and black as the colors of the men. We thus
have white points one to twelve and black points one to twelve.
These two groups of twelve points are subdivided by the bar
into two sets of six each. The name "bar" derives from the fact
that most backgammon boards fold into a box with one side
along this dividing line. As a result, when the box is opened for
play there is actually a bar dividing the points into sets of six
each. The board is thus divided into four parts which (as indicated in Diagram I-1) are named "White Inner Table," "Black
Inner Table," "White Outer Table," and "Black Outer Table."
The word "board" is used interchangeably with the word "table"
by some players; we thus have "White Inner Board," etc.

Before play is begun the thirty men are placed upon the board
in the positions shown in this diagram. During the play you move
your men around the board from your adversary's inner table to
his outer table, to your own outer table, and then to your own
inner table. That is to say, the white men move in the direction

of the arrow in Diagram I-1 and the black men move in the opposite direction. Of course, this arrow, the table names, and the point numbers will not appear on your board. They are put on the diagrams merely for your convenience. Throughout this book you will be White, playing the white men.

Backgammon is an old game. Certainly it is older than all card games and possibly older even than chess. It is, after all, a dice game and dice have been used since the dawn of civilization. Backgammon sets are made of all types of materials and quality. They range from very cheap to very expensive. While the quality of your game depends in no way upon the quality of your set, the amount of satisfaction you derive from playing with it may. Once you have learned the game, it is time to consider buying a reasonably good set. But do not go overboard as a starter, thinking it will make the game easier to play.

The two players roll their dice alternately. Your objective in backgammon is to move your men around the board (subject to certain restrictions on play imposed by the laws) in accordance with the numbers uppermost on the two dice that you roll when it is your turn to play. There is some luck in backgammon but it is by no means all luck. There is also a lot of skill involved. In fact there is so much skill involved that nine of the eighteen major backgammon tournaments played since such events became popular have been won by three men.* There is enough luck in it so that three of the other nine winners have been rather poor players who just happened to get into a lucky streak of the dice.

You start a play by placing your dice in a cup, shaking it, and rolling the dice out onto the space to your right of the bar. If you roll before your adversary has completed his play you must rethrow the dice. If your dice do not come to rest flat upon the table (that is, if they are cocked) they must also be rethrown. Once the dice have come to rest you should leave them alone while you advance your men the exact number of points they indicate. The men are never moved backwards. You may advance any man the number of points indicated by one die and a second man the number of points indicated by the other die, or you may advance any one man for the total number of points the dice indicate. A man can only be advanced to "an open point," that

---

*Publisher's note: Walter Cooke has won two. Tim Holland has won three. Oswald Jacoby has won four.

is, to a point which is not occupied by two, or more, of your opponent's men. In other words, you may advance a man to any point which is unoccupied, to one which has at most one of your opponent's men on it (as will be discussed shortly), or to one on which one or more of your own men sit. When a double is thrown you must make four plays of that number. These plays may be made by advancing one, two, three, or four separate men as you choose—the only condition being that the final combination of advances must total four moves of the number on the dice. Note that in moving a man more than the number of points indicated by a single die it must be possible for that man to touch down temporarily upon an open point. As an example, suppose that your opponent (Black) starts the game (we will return to opening plays shortly) with a 3-1 and advances one of the men on his eight point to his five point with the 3 and uses the 1 to advance a man from his six point to the same five point. See Diagram I-2. When you move a second man to a point upon

Diagram I-2

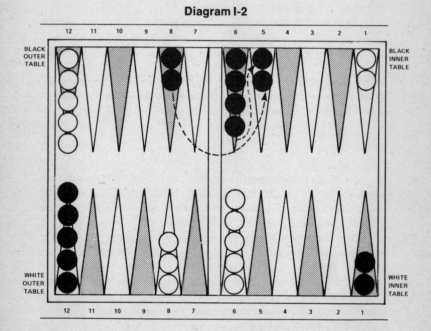

which you already have one man you are said to "make that point." Such points are very helpful to you—they are available for you to use but, as long as you keep at least two men on a point, you deny the use of that point to the enemy. Points upon which your opponent has two or more men act to impede your progress in a similar manner.

Suppose you now roll double 5. You cannot advance either of your "back men" (the two men you have on Black's one point). Regardless of the fact that Black's eleven point is open, the fact that he has more than one man on his six point prevents either of these men from advancing. They have no open point to touch down on as they move forward. On the other hand, if instead of a double 5 you had thrown a 6-4 you could, if you so desired, advance one of your back men to Black's eleven point since that man could use the 6 to touch down at the open black seven point (which is known as the "bar point") while en route. When you have finished moving your men **and** have picked up your dice you have completed your play and it is your adversary's turn to roll.

As a matter of interest note that you start the game controlling your own six and eight points and Black's one and twelve points. Black's men occupy points symmetrically opposed to yours. He has control of his six and eight points and your one and twelve points. There is no limit to the number of your own men that you may place upon any point but you cannot place one of your men, even temporarily, on a point controlled by your opponent—that is, on a point which he has made by occupying it with two or more of his men.

In addition to the above, there are several other requirements which must be met when it is your turn to play. You must play both of the numbers that you roll (all four numbers in the case of doublets) when at all possible. You may play either number first, but you cannot select one number and play it in such a manner that it becomes impossible to play the other one. In other words, you must play both numbers if you can do so. If you can play either of two numbers (but cannot play both numbers) you must play the larger one.

Let us assume that you did roll a 6-4 and did advance one of your back men to Black's eleven point as shown in Diagram I-3. A single man on a point is known as a "blot." You now have blots on Black's one and eleven points. Blots are vulnerable to attack. If your opponent should happen to throw a number which permits him to move one of his men to the point occupied by

Diagram I-3

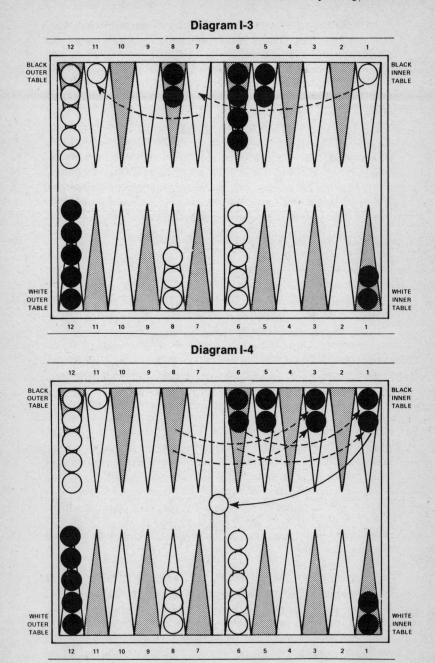

Diagram I-4

one of your blots (in this example he needs a 2 to advance a man to the black eleven point) and if he chooses to make this move, he will be said to have "hit your blot." When he has hit your blot he picks up your man and "places it on the bar." Suppose, instead of throwing a 2, Black throws double 5 (see Diagram I-4). Double 5 is not usually much of a roll except as a freight mover: it does get men around the board. But right now it has become deadly. He will use two of his 5's to hit your blot on his one point (and simultaneously make this point) with two men on his six point, and the other two 5's to make his three point (with the two men left on his eight point). Black now controls blocks on his one, three, five, and six points—the only open points in his inner table are the two and four points—and you have a man on the bar plus a blot on the black eleven point!

Whenever you have one or more men on the bar the laws place a severe restriction on your play. You must bring all the men that you have on the bar into your opponent's inner table before you can move any other man. This isn't much of a restriction in the starting position (Diagram I-1). The only point your opponent holds in his inner table is the six point, so you can play any number from the bar except double 6. Once he makes a second point, such as the five point, he blocks off three more rolls (double 5 and 6-5). Why do we say three more rolls? Because any regular roll such as 6-5 is actually two different rolls (6 with one die and 5 with the other die or 5 with the first die and 6 with the second die). If he makes a third point in his inner table, that cuts out five more possibilities and leaves you with just twenty-seven playable rolls out of the thirty-six that are possible. A fourth point made leaves you with just twenty playable rolls. A fifth point made leaves just eleven. If he has all six points made you can't play at all until he breaks one of them.

Thus it is not a matter of life and death to expose a blot when your opponent holds one, two, or even three points in his inner table—but it is when he holds more than three. Therefore, the time to take chances with blots is early in the game. You may have to later on, but if you do you should be fully aware of the danger.

In the example we are looking at (Diagram I-4), you exposed two blots when your opponent held two points in his inner table. He has rolled double 5, hit one of your blots, and made two more points in his inner table. He now holds four points and is said to have made a "four point board."

You must roll a 2 or 4 to play at all. If you roll some usually good roll such as double 1, you lose your whole play and are in dire straits. You have a second blot exposed on the black eleven point; if your enemy hits it you will have two men on the bar and there will be a good chance he will make the other two points in his inner table before you can enter them both. If he does he will have closed you out until such time as he gets around to bearing off his men (see below).

Now let's look at Diagram I-5. We don't show all of the men here

Diagram I-5

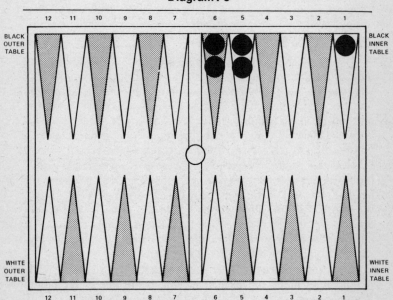

because the important considerations have to do with your man on the bar and the black men in their inner table. You roll 3-1. You can enter on either the one or the three point. In general you will come in on the one point in order to hit his blot, and play the 3 by advancing your man to the black four point or by moving one of your other men three points. There are, however, situations where you will enter with the 3, use the 1 for some purpose other than entering, and refuse to hit the blot at all.

Fundamental strategy requires that you pay special attention to blots (both yours and Black's). You don't want to hit a blot merely because it is there, but you always want to consider the possibility. You don't want to expose a blot for the sheer joy of living dangerously but you don't want to walk around wearing suspenders and a belt and carrying safety pins in your pockets. The more points you have made the more mobile your position and the less mobile your opponent's. You can make a point by moving two men to it but it is far easier to make a point by just adding one man to a blot you already have there.

If you have to leave a blot when your opponent has made several points in his inner table, leave your man where he is exposed to the smallest number of shots. In general, when open to a direct shot (when you can be hit with one of the numbers from 1 to 6) the closer you are to the danger the less the chance of being hit; while when open to an indirect, or long, shot (7 or more) the further away the safer. Also, the chance of being hit by any indirect shot is less than the chance of being hit by any direct shot.

A second, and more important, guideline is that when you must expose a blot, expose it on the point that will be of most value to you if the blot lives. (See Lesson IV, page 55, Diagram 14, as a simple example.)

As already mentioned, once play has begun the players roll and play alternately. How do you determine who plays first? Obviously, you could cut cards, toss a coin, roll high dice, or use any other method you wish to separate the "firsts" from the "seconds." Backgammon rules provide for an easy, straightforward way to accomplish this. After the board has been set up and the seats chosen, each player rolls a single die. If there is a tie the two dice are picked up and rerolled. The player rolling the higher number makes the first move by advancing his men just as though he had won the toss of a coin and rolled both dice himself.

We stated earlier that, "Your objective in backgammon is to move your men around the board." We would have been more accurate if we had said, "Your object in backgammon is, first, to move your men around the board until you have **all** of them in your own inner table and, second, to "bear them off" before your enemy is able to "bear off" all of his men. If you succeed in bearing off all of your men before your opponent bears off all of his men you have won the game and, if you are playing for a stake, you have won that stake. If when you bear off your last man your opponent has not borne off a single man you have won a gammon and the stake, if any, is doubled. Further, if when you bear off your last man your opponent not only has not borne off a single man but has one or more men in your inner table or on the bar, you have won a backgammon and the stake, if any, is tripled.

It is now apparent that the rules governing play must cover three different possibilities, namely, forward movement of the men, entering from the bar, and bearing off. We have discussed the first two of these and it now remains to discuss the third.

Assume your men are positioned as shown in Diagram I-6. In this situation, where the enemy has no men in your inner table

Diagram I-6

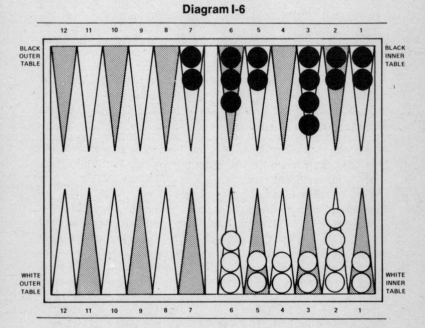

or on the bar, the position of his men has no bearing whatsoever on your play. You simply "bear off" (that is, remove from the board) your men as rapidly as the rules will permit. You may play either number first. Having thrown the dice, you may bear off a man on a point corresponding to the number uppermost on a die or you may advance a man the number of points indicated by that number. Of course, both numbers must be played. At times this may prove to be a serious disadvantage. In the event you roll a number which is, at the time you play it, higher than the number of any point upon which you have men remaining you must bear off a man from your highest numbered occupied point.

Returning now to Diagram I-6, assume that you roll double 5. You have two men on the five point so you bear them off as two of your four plays. For the remaining two plays you have no choice. You must move two of your men from your six point to the one point. You have no other legal play available at this point. You cannot bear a man off from the four point with a 5 when you have a man on your six point. You could, of course, have moved three men from your six point and borne off one of your men on the five point but this would not make sense. You want to bear your men off as rapidly as possible.

Diagram I-7

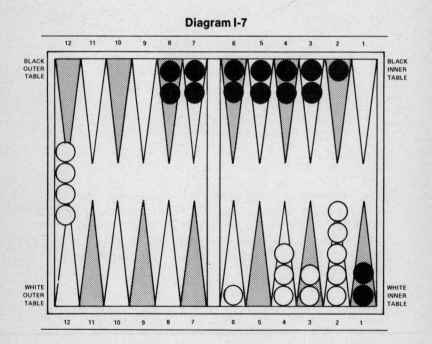

Take a look at Diagram I-7. You are well along in the process of bearing off and Black still has two men left on your one point. At your last roll you were forced to leave a blot (notice that lone man on your six point). Obviously, Black failed to hit it and now you want to get that blot out of trouble right away. You are surely going to win the game if Black never hits one of your blots but you are quite likely to lose if he does hit one. You roll 6-3. Your first thought is to use the 6 to bear off that man on your six point. Then you will have to play the 3 and the only way you can play it would be to bear off a man from the three point and leave the other one exposed as a blot. Black will have another chance to hit you.

Can you protect yourself? Yes, you can! You are allowed to play either number first, so start your play by using the 3 to move that man from the six point to the three point. Then you can use the 6 to bear off one of the men on your four point. This play may be slightly confusing, but it is proper and legal.

We have by no means gone into all of the intricacies of bearing off —we have only barely covered the laws governing it. We'll return to it in Lesson X.

You should get in the habit of shaking your dice well before you roll them, but it is even more important to hold back your roll until your opponent has completed his play by starting to pick up his dice. Argument after argument is caused by premature rolls. Incidentally, while very few people use just one pair of dice it would avoid this source of argument, since when just one pair are used the play is completed when the man who has rolled picks up the dice and hands them to his opponent.

As we have said, in all the diagrams in this book White will be moving his men in a counterclockwise direction and Black in the opposite, or clockwise, direction. This is immaterial in backgammon. The men could be set up with the inner tables to the left. As a matter of fact the laws suggest that the home (inner) tables be nearer the source of light. However, when learning get used to going just one way. Later on it will be up to you to learn to move the other way.

Unless you have already played backgammon, or some similar game such as the Navy's acey-deucy, you will have considerable difficulty in just moving your men around the board. We suggest that until you have acquired the knack of moving men without counting 1, 2, 3, 4, 5, etc., that you just roll and move men around the board. Note that a move of exactly six always brings a man from a point in one table to the corresponding point in the next table; that an even number moves a man to a point of the same color as the point he just left while an odd number moves a man to a point of the opposite color.

So much for the principal rules governing play. In subsequent lessons we shall examine the options open to you under various conditions, and develop your appreciation of the fine points involved as well as fundamental strategy. In general, after you have thrown your dice and before you play, think a moment. Look to see if you can make a point or hit a blot. You may not want to do either but make sure you haven't overlooked the possibility. Don't play too safe but, at the same time, don't expose blots for the sheer joy of gambling. Get your back men off and running at the earliest possible opportunity and impede the progress of your opponent's back men as much as possible.

Lesson II

THE RUNNING GAME

If you have followed our suggestion in Lesson I you will have spent some time in just moving your men around the board to familiarize yourself with how they move. You will probably have played some games right to the end and will have seen that at some point in the play all the white and black men will have passed each other. As soon as this occurs you are said to be in a "running game." In the early and middle stages of a game you don't get into a running game by accident. If you do get there, at some time or other either you or your opponent has deliberately moved into that position.

Why does a player do this? Because, when his estimate of the existing situation shows that he is closer to winning than his opponent, he will want to eliminate the possibility of having to leave a blot for his opponent to hit and will, therefore, break contact when he can.

Why are we discussng the running game before giving the proper opening moves and replies to them? Because we want you to know something about swimming before you get into the water. If you disagree with this, skip to Lessons III and IV; but if you want to get the most value out of them, read this lesson first.

Diagram II-1 shows a typical running game position. There is still some contact between your men on Black's twelve point and his men on your twelve point but there is no real chance that either of you will ever have to expose a blot to the other. Which of you has the advantage here? It is your roll and that is in your

Diagram II-1

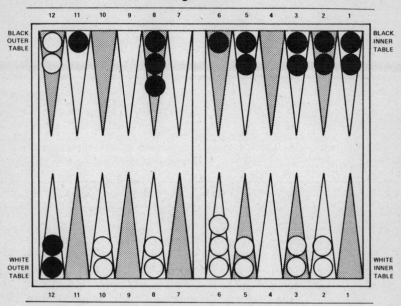

favor but if you look the position over carefully you will see that Black has a slightly better game.

How do you come to this conclusion? In this position it is a cinch to count how many pips you are ahead or behind. A pip is one of those little spots on the dice. If you roll a 6 you advance a man six pips. If you roll double 4 you advance one to four men a total of sixteen pips.

Your pip count is the total number of pips you would have to roll (assuming no waste motion) to bring all of your men around to your inner table and then bear them off. Obviously, there is going to be some wastage but in most positions you can just assume that this will affect your opponent as much as it will affect you.

You don't need to make total pip counts to see how far you are ahead or behind. You can count the net difference if you wish. Now back to our position to demonstrate this. You have the same number of men in your inner table as Black has in his and if you moved two of the men on your six point forward to your one point (a total move of ten pips) your inner boards would be identical. The positions in the outer tables would also be identical if you took one of your men on your ten point and moved it one pip back to the eleven point and moved the other man on your ten point two pips forward to your eight point.

Hence you are $10 + 2 - 1 = 11$ pips behind, but it is your roll. You could roll double 6 and be thirteen pips ahead or 2-1 and still be eight pips behind, but you don't know what you are going to roll.

Your average roll, when you allow for the extra moves with doublets, is 8-1/6 pips.

How did this position develop? Prior to his last roll two of the black men now on the black eight point were on your bar point. He rolled double 5 and moved tentatively to this position.

How do you make a tentative move? You move and leave your dice on the table. It is not necessary to say you are moving tentatively but it is good form to do so. Anyway Black did this and finally picked up his dice to show he had made his play.

Did Black make a pip count before picking up his dice? Maybe he did, but probably he just saw that he could not afford to leave those two men back on your bar point where it would be very difficult to get them away safely later on.

How should the play go from here on? Each player should endeavor to bring his men into his inner table as quickly as possible and to bear them off in that same manner. Since it is White's roll and his outside men are in about the same position as Black's, White is likely to get the first men off. Later on Black's inner table position will let him bear men off with a 1 while White's won't.

Most running games do not develop as such for quite a while. Still it is possible to get into one after only two moves by each player. Look at Diagram II-2. Each player has started with two rolls of 6-5 and brought his two back men out. The player about to roll has a minuscule advantage and is said to be a half roll ahead.

This is not going to be a very interesting game but there will be a best way to play most rolls and we will actually play it in Lesson IX to show some running game techniques.

You got into the preceding running game without any effort on anyone's part. Other running game positions may be reached this way or because one player tries to work into one.

Diagram II-2

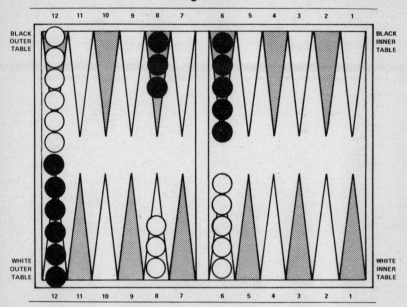

Why does he do this? Because in his opinion he will have the best of the game once there are no worries about blots being hit. How does he know that he will have the best of it? The expert way is by means of a pip count. In positions like that shown in Diagram II-1 it is easy to count the net difference. In most other positions it will be more difficult. Appendix A shows how to make an accurate pip count. Look at it now if you wish, but don't work on it yet.

Some backgammon teachers have recommended a 4-3-2-1 count to make a quick running game estimate (4 for each man in the adverse inner table; 3 for each man in the adverse outer table; 2 for each man in your own outer table; and 1 for each man in your own inner table).

We are great believers in the 4-3-2-1 count in bridge but it doesn't work well in backgammon. Take the position shown in Diagram II-3 as an example.

Your count is nine for the three men on the black twelve point, eight for your four men on your eight point, and eight for the eight men you have in your inner table, for a total of twenty-five.

Diagram II-3

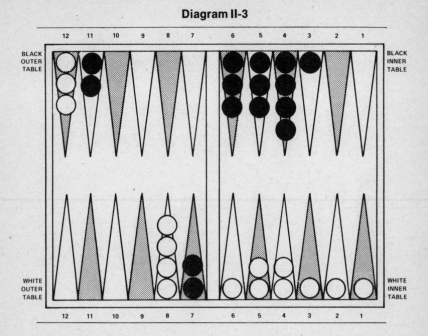

Black's count is six for his two men on your bar point, four for his two men on his own eleven point, and eleven for the eleven men in his inner table, for a total of twenty-one.

Now put the backgammon player's eye to work. You note that it takes just one pip to move your men from the black twelve point to your outer table while it will take Black six pips to get his men from your bar point to his outer table; that it takes just two pips to move your men from your eight point to your inner table while it will take Black five pips to get his men from his eleven point to his inner table. You also note that your men in the inner table are more advanced than Black's. You arrive at the conclusion that at the present moment the positions are about even—with possibly a slight edge in your favor.

Your backgammon player's eye has worked better than the 4-3-2-1 count, but it hasn't told the whole story. Actually you are nine pips ahead and it is your roll.

It is also apparent that the position shown in Diagram II-3 is by no means a running game. There is still plenty of contact. The two black men on your bar point and your three men on the

Diagram II-4

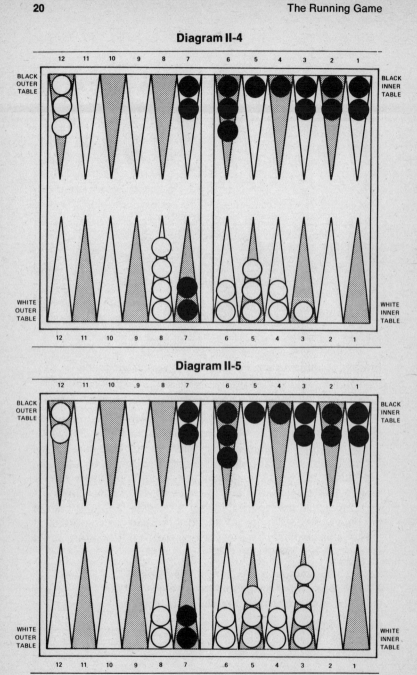

Diagram II-5

black twelve point must pass one another and, until they do, you will have contact.

Then why do we show this position at all in a lesson on the running game? Because it is your roll and you roll double 5. You have already analyzed the position and seen that it is about even. The double 5 puts you well ahead. You simply move your three men from the black twelve point (two to your eight point; one to your three point) and start a running game. In addition to being ahead, you have another advantage: you can expect to get the first man off. Your six men outside your inner table are on your eight point—each is just two pips from home. Both of Black's men on your bar point are twelve pips from home and the two men he has on his eleven point are five pips away.

Diagram II-4 shows a situation somewhat similar to that in Diagram II-3. Your inside men have been moved back a trifle. Also, Black's men have been moved forward somewhat. The two men that were on his eleven point have been advanced to his bar point and the men in his inner table have been advanced so that the resulting positions will be about equal after you have played your double 5.

If you want to maintain contact you move three men to your three point to produce the position shown in Diagram II-5. If you want to shift to a running game (which is still the proper play for you to make) you simply advance your three men from Black's twelve point.

There are two reasons for this. The first is that while your running game will be almost even (Black will have a slight edge because it is his roll) you will probably get the first men off. The second is that if you maintain contact you are more likely to have to leave a blot than your opponent. In a fairly even position the man who has to give his opponent a shot at a blot becomes a decided underdog.

Now let us look at two more situations, those in Diagrams II-6 and II-7. It is your roll and you have rolled double 5. What should you do?

In this first case, Diagram II-6, it would be very foolish to run. Not only will you be very far behind in the resulting running game but, if you do wait, you are extremely likely to get a shot at a black blot. You will even get cracks at two blots if he throws a 5-1, 4-2, or 4-1.

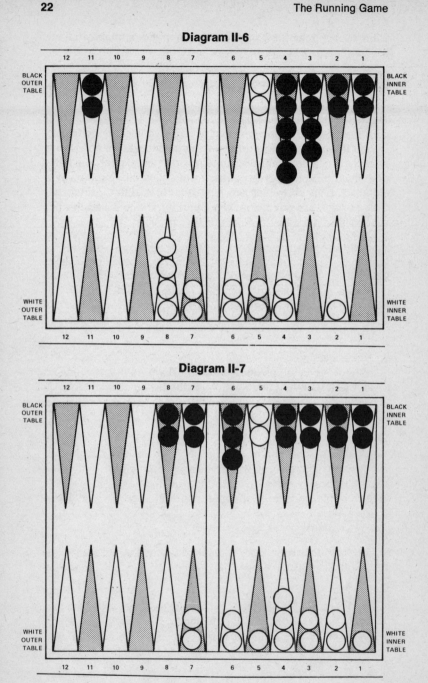

Diagram II-6

Diagram II-7

In the second case, Diagram II-7, there is no point in waiting. As far as the probability of blots is concerned, you will have all the worst of it if you wait. On the other hand, if you run with your two men on the black five point you will be only slightly behind in the running game.

We are going to keep coming back to the running game in almost every lesson that follows. You must have a game plan at all times. That game plan should be to try to get into a running game when you are ahead, to get further behind in an effort to maintain contact when you are behind, and to maintain all options when you are slightly ahead or slightly behind. In other words, be ready to get off and running with big dice and to sit back and wait with little numbers.

Lesson III

THE FIRST MOVE

The player who wins the first move starts the game. It is an advantage; not much of an advantage to be sure, but an advantage.

Except in some way-out variations of backgammon you don't start with a double number, so we are going to discuss the fifteen possible regular rolls here and let the play of opening doublets go until later on.

In Lesson I we recommended that after rolling, and before playing, you should always look to see if: (a) you can hit a blot, or (b) you can make a point.

You can't hit a blot on the first play: your opponent's men are all safe on points which he controls, but you do have five rolls that allow you to make a point. These are:

6-1 You can make your bar point by moving one man from the black twelve point with the 6 and one man from your eight point with the 1. See Diagram III-1.

3-1 You can make your five point by moving one man from your eight point with the 3 and one man from your six point with the 1. See Diagram III-2.

4-2 You can make your four point by moving one man from your eight point with the 4 and one man from your six point with the 2. See Diagram III-3.

Diagram III-1

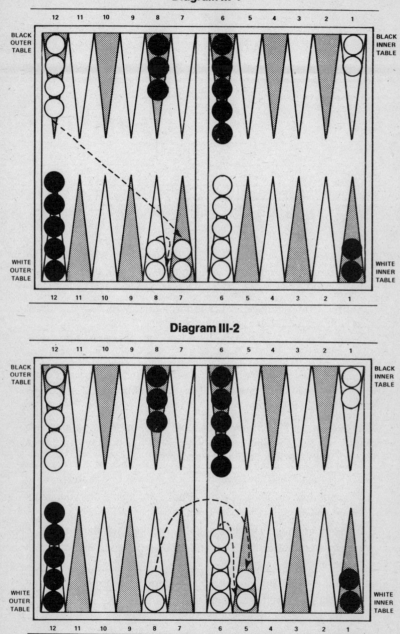

Diagram III-3

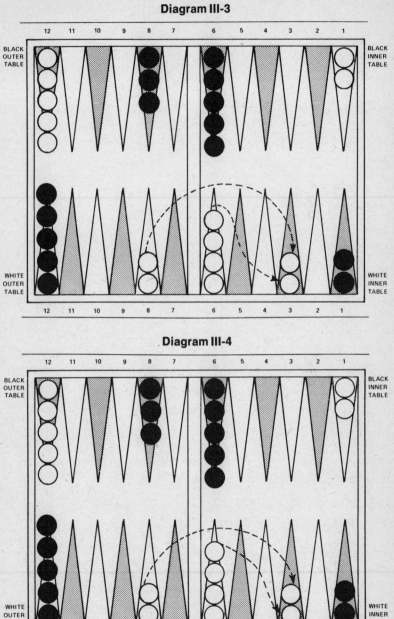

Diagram III-4

Diagram III-5

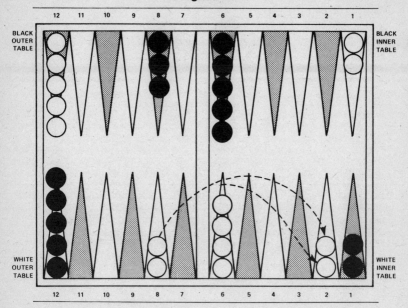

5-3   You can make your three point by moving one man from your
       eight point with the 5 and one man from your six point with
       the 3. See Diagram III-4.

6-4   You can make your two point by moving one man from your
       eight point with the 6 and one man from your six point with
       the 4. See Diagram III-5.

With the first three of these point-making rolls you have no
problem. You make your bar point with your 6-1; your five point
with your 3-1; and your four point with your 4-2—whether you
are a beginner, an average player, or a great expert.

But we have an alternate choice, which we shall discuss shortly,
with 5-3. When it comes to 6-4, whether you are a beginner or
an expert, you should **not** make the two point. Those men on the
two point will be almost entirely out of play. It is a cinch for your
adversary to move past them to your three, four, or five point.
Remember what we said in Lesson I—you should not make a
point merely because it is there for the making.

Basic Opening Moves

6-5 This is known as "lover's leap." Move one of your back men
     from the black one point to the black twelve point, where he
     joins the five men already there. This is a good roll, since it
     starts you well on your way to a successful game. See Dia-
     gram III-6.

Diagram III-6

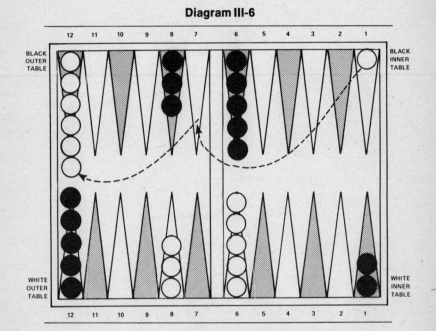

6-4 Move one of your back men from the black one point to the
     black eleven point. He is exposed to a direct 2 but you have
     lost little if he is hit and, if he is not hit, he is in a beautiful
     position to move to your outer table on your next roll. Do not
     make the two point with 6-4. See Diagram III-7.

6-3 Move one of your back men from the black one point to the
     black ten point. There is no way to avoid leaving a blot no
     matter how you play the roll. See Diagram III-8.

6-2 Again we run with a back man from the black one point. There
     is no way to play this number safely. See Diagram III-9.

Diagram III-7

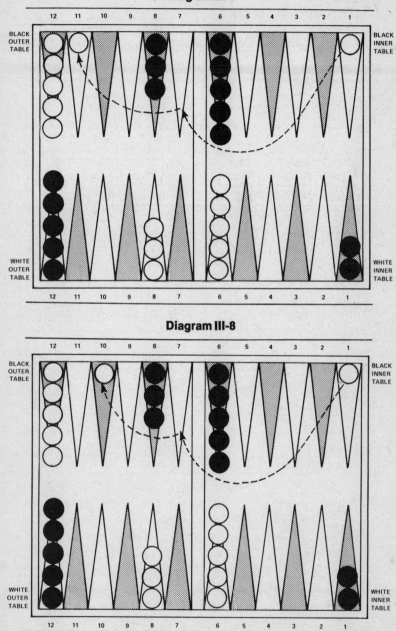

Diagram III-8

Diagram III-9

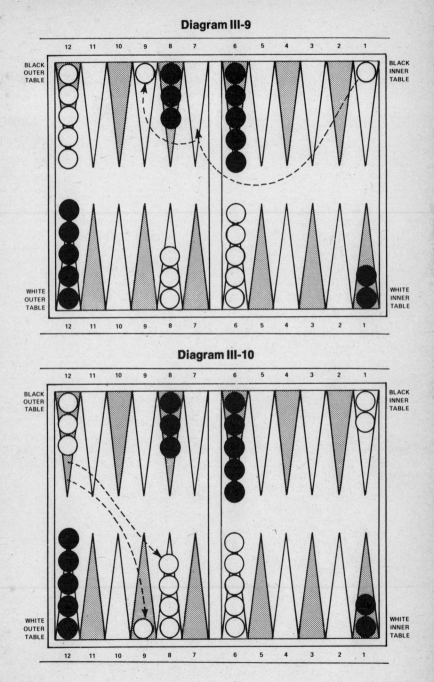

Diagram III-10

Diagram III-11

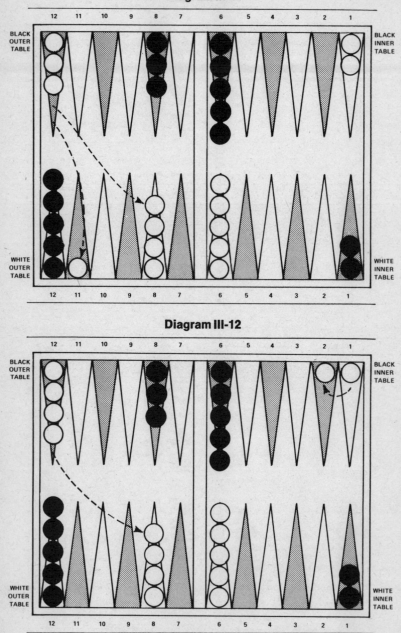

Diagram III-12

Diagram III-13

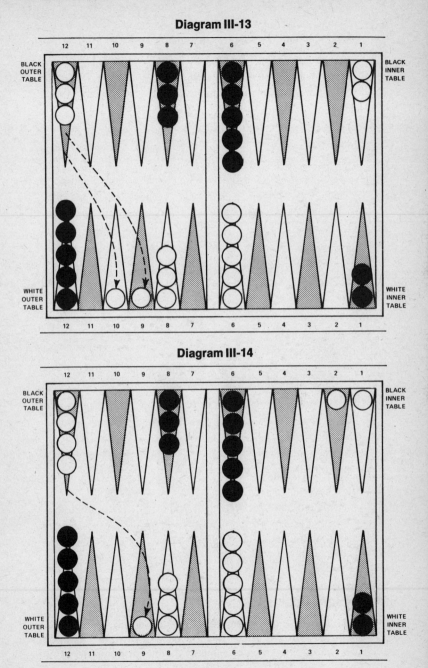

Diagram III-14

6-1   Make your bar point. See Diagram III-1.

5-4   Move two men from the black twelve point to your eight and
       nine points. The man on the nine point is exposed to 5-3, 6-2,
       double 4, and double 2, but don't worry about this. It is a risk
       you can well afford since you have put that man in good posi-
       tion for your next turn. See Diagram III-10.

5-3   Make your three point. See Diagram III-4.

5-2   Move two men from the black twelve point to your eight and
       eleven points. See Diagram III-11.

5-1   Move a man from the black twelve point to your eight point
       with the 5 and one of your back men from the black one point
       to the black two point with the 1. See Diagram III-12.

4-3   Move two of your men from the black twelve point to your
       nine and ten points. You are exposing two blots to indirect
       shots but your opponent cannot hit both of them. In fact, the
       odds are well over two to one that he won't be able to hit
       either of them. If he doesn't, you will have two valuable
       builders bearing on those very important five and bar points.
       See Diagram III-13.

4-2   Make your four point. See Diagram III-3.

4-1   This move is similar to the move with the 5-1, in that you use
       the 4 to move one of your men from the black twelve point
       and the 1 to move one of your back men from the black one
       point to the black two point. See Diagram III-14.

3-2   This is the same kind of move as with 4-3. Move two of your
       men from the black twelve point around the corner to your
       outer table where they will bear on the five and bar points.
       See Diagram III-15.

3-1   No problem here! Make your five point. See Diagram III-2.

2-1   This move is similar to that of 5-1 and 4-1. Move one of your
       men from the black twelve point to your eleven point with the
       2 and one of your back men from the black one point to the
       black two point with the 1. See Diagram III-16.

More About Opening Moves

You do not have to spend any time thinking about 6-5, 6-1, 4-2,
and 3-1. These are all good first moves and no one has been
able to suggest any ways of playing them that compare at all

Diagram III-15

Diagram III-16

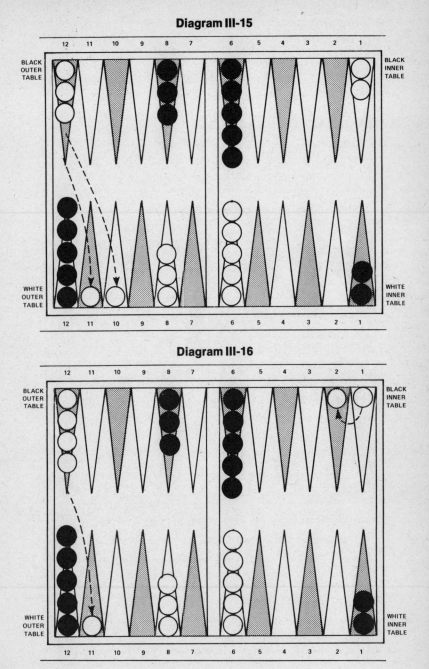

favorably with the standard ones. Let's take a second look at the other rolls now.

6-4   The basic plays just discussed for these three rolls are the
6-3   traditional plays. In the last fifteen years the experts have
6-2   experimented with an entirely different kind of play here.
       Instead of running all the way with one of the back men on
       the black one point they merely use the 6 to move him to the
       black bar point and use the 4, 3, or 2 (as the case may be)
       to move a man from the black twelve point to the appropriate
       point in the white outer table. See Diagram III-17.

Diagram III-17

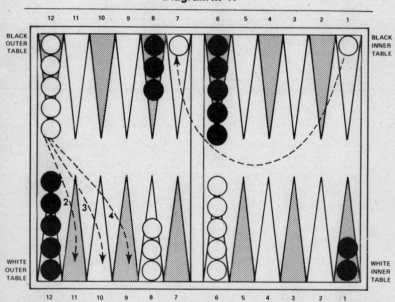

This alternate play has considerable merit with 6-2 and some merit with 6-3. But it has practically no merit with 6-4; its proponents have practically abandoned it, so our recommendation to you is not to use it at all.

6-2   There happens to be a special play with 6-2. It is decidedly
       an attacking play and one that we have always favored. It is
       to move a man from the black twelve point all the way to your
       five point. See Diagram III-18. We are delighted to report that

Diagram III-18

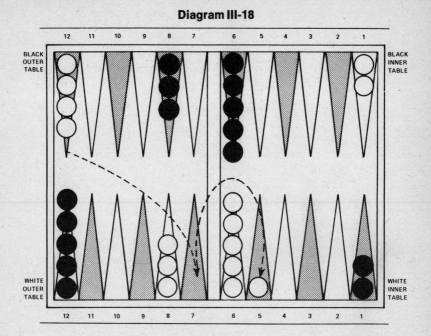

it has gained almost universal expert acceptance today and we recommend that you experiment with this play as soon as you get out of the beginner class.

5-4 Stick with the basic play shown in Diagram III-10. The alternate one, which is to move one of your back men from the black one point to the black ten point, is not recommended.

5-3 The basic play shown in Diagram III-4 is best. For a while the experts tried an alternate play, which was to move two men from the black twelve point to their eight and ten points. See Diagram III-19. A few still make this alternate play but most of the others, including the writers, have gone back to making the three point.

5-2 The basic play shown in Diagram III-11 is the only good play here but you may want to try a couple of others. We will discuss them here but they really aren't worth trying.

The first bad play is to move to the position shown in Diagram III-20. When Oswald Jacoby first learned to play backgammon over forty years ago he was taught to move a man from the black twelve point to his own six point. The instructor

Diagram III-19

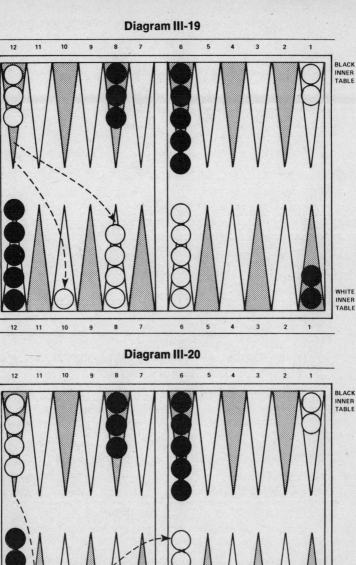

Diagram III-20

said, "You are advancing a man with complete safety." He learned to beat the instructor with regularity and one reason he beat him was that it didn't take him long to see that this kind of play was for the birds.

At first he experimented with what turned out to be another bad way to play 5-2. This ineffective way was to move one of the back men from the black one point to the black three point with the 2 and one of the men from the black twelve point to his own eight point with the 5. See Diagram III-21.

Diagram III-21

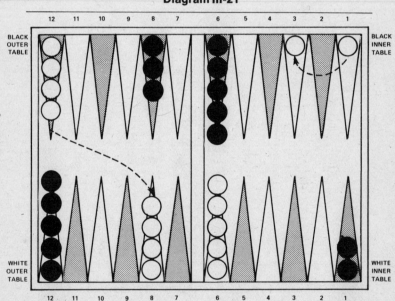

There was nothing wrong with the move of the 5. It was the split of the two back men to the three and one points that caused trouble. If his opponent rolled double 5 he would hit both blots while making his one and three points. Jacoby would have to bring two men back in from the bar against a three point board. One time in four he would do this and have a playable, but poor, game. The rest of the time he

would bring neither, or just one, in and have an almost
hopeless game!

5-1   The alternate play here is to use your 1 to expose a man on
      your own five point. It has some merit but we much prefer the
      standard use of the 1—move a back man from the black one
      point to the black two point as shown in Diagram III-12.

4-3   The basic play shown in Diagram III-13 is still recommended
      but there are several others that have some merit. The best of
      these is to use the 4 to move a man from the black twelve
      point to your nine point and the 3 to move a back man from
      the black one point to the black four point. See Diagram
      III-22.

Diagram III-22

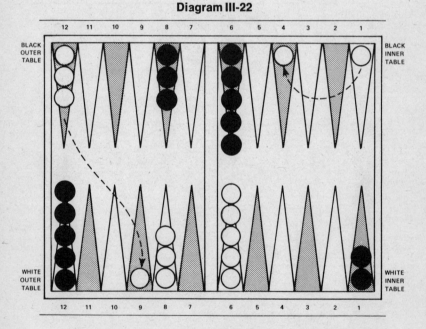

How about the play of moving a man to your own ten point
with the 3 and one of your back men from the black one point
to the black five point with the 4? We do consider it, but we
reject it! Try to avoid exposing a blot on your opponent's
five point. It is bad enough if he makes this valuable point;

it is terrible if he makes it and puts one of your men on the bar at the same time.

4-1   The basic play is the best. An alternate used occasionally by players who like to attack recklessly is to use the 4 as in the basic play and the 1 to expose a blot on the five point. See Diagram III-23. When this play works it is wonderful but the

Diagram III-23

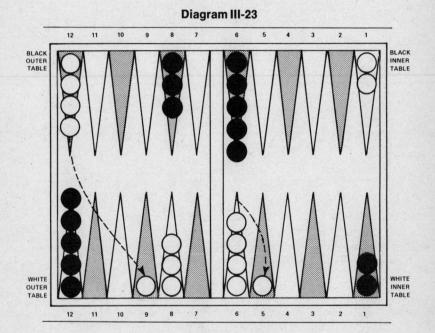

trouble with it is that, in addition to the many rolls that will hit your blot on the five point, 6-2 or 5-3 will hit your blot on the nine point. Also, with double 2 he can hit both blots (but will probably settle for just hitting one of them); with double 4 he *will* hit both blots.

3-2   The same general principles apply as with 4-3. Do not consider the absolutely safe play of moving a man from the black twelve point to your eight point. There is, however, an acceptable alternate play which is to use 2 as before (by moving a man from the black twelve point to your eleven point)

Diagram III-24

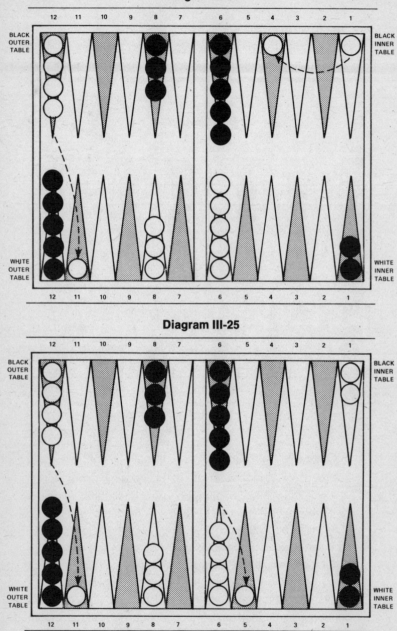

and the 3 to move a back man from the black one point to the black four point. See Diagram III-24.

2-1 As with 5-1 and 4-1 the alternate play is to use the 1 to expose a blot on your five point. See Diagram III-25. As with the others it is not the sort of alternate you want to use as a steady diet.

Lesson IV

THE REPLY TO THE
FIRST MOVE

Your reply to the first move, as well as your reply to all subsequent moves, has to be based in large measure on what your opponent has already played. Let's see how you play each of the six doublets in case you are lucky enough to roll one of them.

Double 1

The best opening roll. It gives you a tremendous position right off the bat. Move two men from your eight point to your bar point and two men from your six point to your five point. Diagram IV-1 shows the position after Black has started with 3-1 and you have replied with double 1.

He has made his five point but you have made your five point and your bar point. Unless he rolls 6-1, 5-2, or 4-3 and hits your blot, you have a very good chance to have four points in a row at your next turn.

If your opponent has rolled 5-1, 4-1, or 2-1 and split his back men you don't make this play. The blot you would have to leave on the eight point would be too vulnerable. Instead you play double 1 like 3-1 to produce the good position shown in Diagram IV-2.

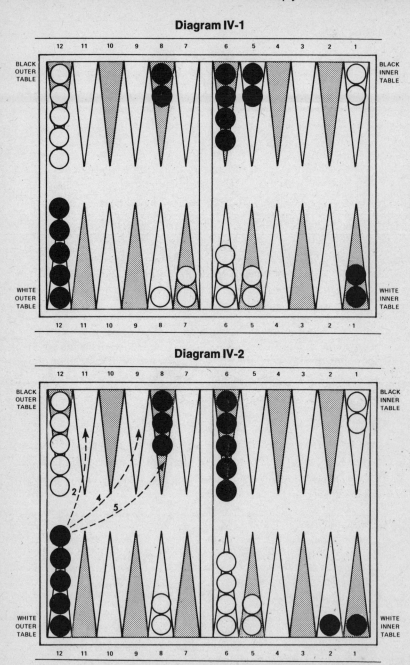

Diagram IV-1

Diagram IV-2

Double 2

Irrespective of what Black's first play has been, use two of your 2's to make your four point. If you can hit a blot with the others, do so; otherwise, move two men from the black twelve point to your eleven point. Diagram IV-3 shows the play after Black has started with 5-4. (Note that you could have used all four 2's to hit his blot but the point-making play is far superior.)

If Black has started with 6-1 you make a slightly different play. You still use two 2's to make your four point, but now you use the other two to move your two back men from the black one point to the black three point.

Double 3

There are more attractive ways to play this fine roll than any other. The reason is that any of your fifteen men can make effective moves of three pips. In general the best way to play it is to make the three and five points in your inner table. Diagram IV-4 shows the position after Black has started with 4-3 and you have made this play. Note that you could have hit the blot on his ten point but you did not.

Suppose Black had started with a 6-3 and moved a man to your ten point. You should use two of your 3's to point on that blot and the other two to make your five point. See Diagram IV-5.

Diagram IV-6 shows how you should play double 3 after Black has started with 5-1, 4-1, or 2-1 and split his back men. You did not make your five point because that would leave a blot on your eight point exposed to either a 6 or a 7.

Double 4

It has been said that you can't play a double 4 badly. This isn't entirely true. An idiot could move four men from his six point to his two point or some other move as nonsensical, but there are any number of good moves.

The best way in most positions is to move two of your back men from the black one point to the black five point and two of your men from the black twelve point to your nine point. Diagram IV-7 shows

Diagram IV-3

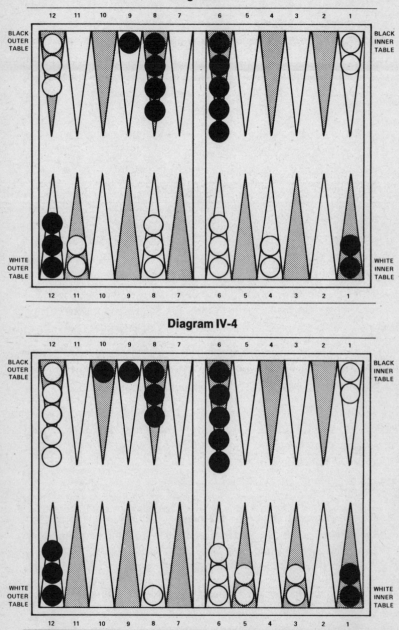

Diagram IV-4

Diagram IV-5

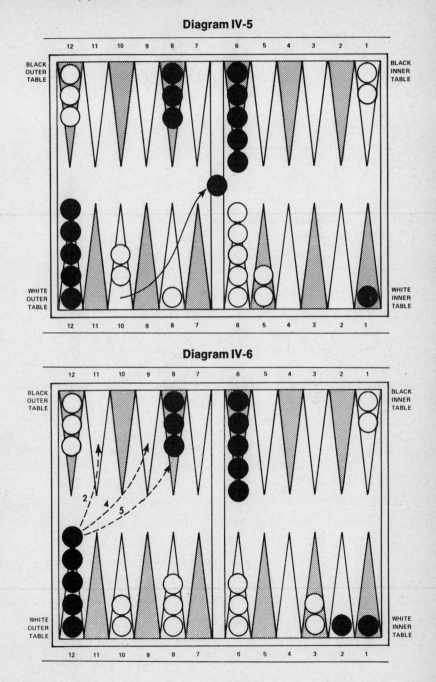

Diagram IV-6

the position after Black has started with a 6-1. You are in a very strong and flexible position. Your men on the black five point bear directly on the black outer table and indirectly on your outer table. Your men on the nine point block some enemy plays and threaten your bar, five, four, and three points.

In case your opponent has advanced one of his back men to your two or four point he has laid himself open to an even stronger play. You move two of your men from your eight point to make your four point and two of your men from your six point to make your two point. In making these two points you will also be hitting a blot and giving your opponent a very bad position. See Diagram IV-8. The only rolls to give him a playable game will be 5-4 or 3-2. With the first he makes your five point; with the second your three point.

Double 5

Unless Black has moved one of the men on your one point the only thing you can do with this roll is to move two men from the black twelve point to your three point.

This is a fairly good move, but if Black has moved one of those back men you can do something really good with double 5. You make your one point with two men from your six point and your three point with two men from your eight point. Diagram IV-9 shows the position after Black started with 6-4 and you have replied with double 5.

Double 6

Unless your opponent has started with 6-1 you make both bar points. Diagram IV-10 shows the position after an opening 6-4 by Black.

You could have hit the blot on your one point but that play would be silly.

Diagrams IV-11 and IV-12 show two ways to play double 6 after Black's 6-1 has blocked your back men. Each play has merit but we slightly favor the play of four men to your bar point (Diagram IV-11).

With rolls other than doublets you tend to play the same as if you were moving first, but there is no roll where there won't be some exception to this general principle.

Diagram IV-7

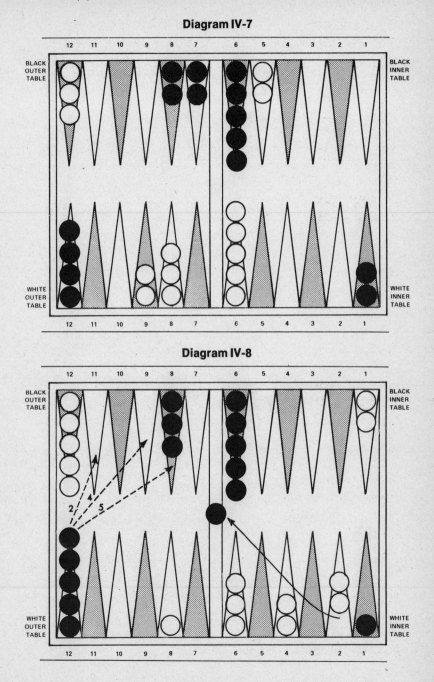

Diagram IV-8

Diagram IV-9

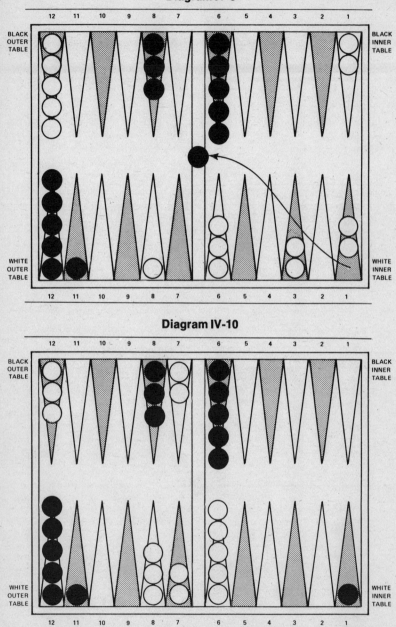

Diagram IV-10

Diagram IV-11

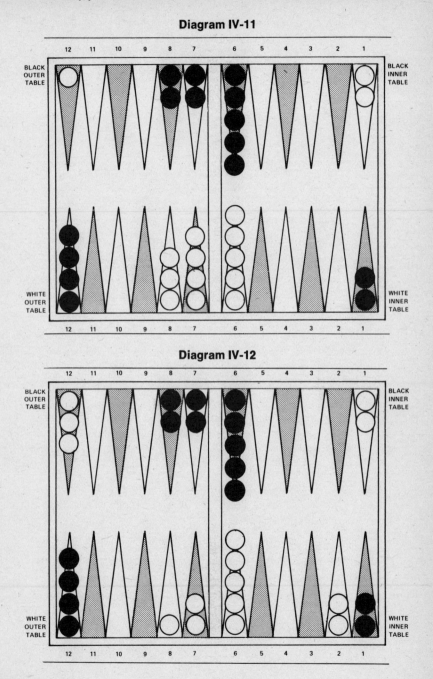

Diagram IV-12

Look to see if your opponent's first play has put a blot where you can hit it or if it has made your normal play either impossible or unattractive. If these conditions do not apply, make your normal play. Now let's look at some of the exceptions.

6-5   Lover's leap cannot be made if your opponent has made his bar point with a 6-1. In fact, except for nonsense moves, you are restricted to one of the two plays shown in Diagrams IV-13 and IV-14.

We strongly recommend the play shown in Diagram IV-14. Your blot is exposed to any 6, or to any combination which adds up to 6, but if it is not hit you will be in a fine position to make your bar point at your next turn. Remember, when you must expose a blot try to expose it where it will do some good if allowed to live.

In case your opponent started with 6-4, 6-3, or 6-2 and used the 6 to move a back man from your one point to your bar point you have a very good way to play 6-5. See Diagram IV-15. You have used the 6 to hit the man on the bar point and the 5 to hit the man on the one point. He has to bring two men in from the bar and even if he hits the blot on your one point you expect to make your bar point at your next turn.

6-4   If your opponent has moved a man into your outer table you
6-3   don't want to make the basic move with either of these plays since your blot in his outer table will be exposed to two direct shots. Of course, if you can hit the blot in your outer table you do so but, if you can't, you solve your problem as shown in Diagrams IV-16 and IV-17. In both cases Black has started with a 6-4.

In Diagram IV-16 you have used the 6-4 to make your two point. Not a happy choice, but the best one available. In Diagram IV-17 you have used 6-3 to move a man from the black twelve point to your four point. This attacking play may pay dividends.

6-2   If Black started with 6-4 and brought one of his back men to your eleven point, hit him with the 2 and use the 6 to move

Diagram IV-13

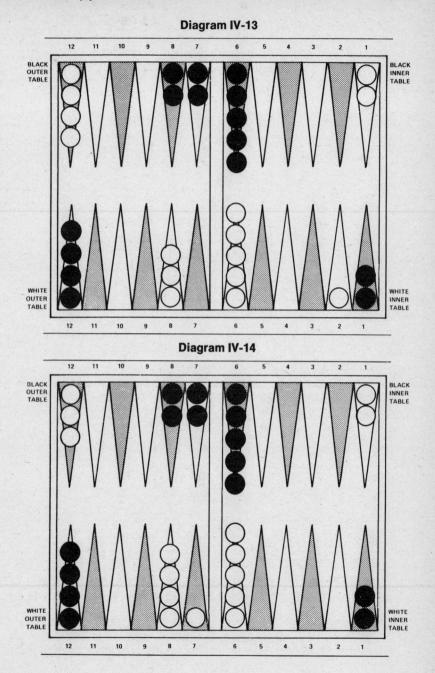

Diagram IV-14

Diagram IV-15

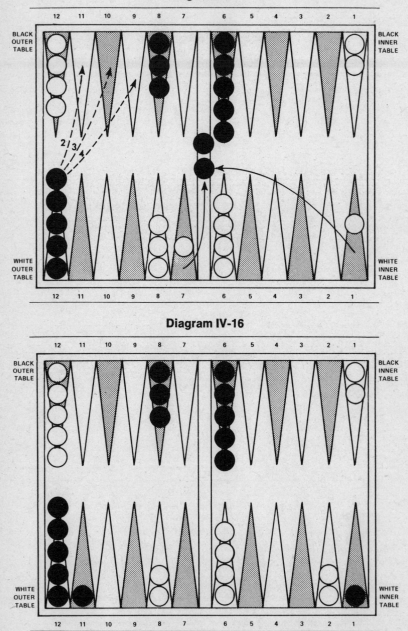

Diagram IV-16

Diagram IV-17

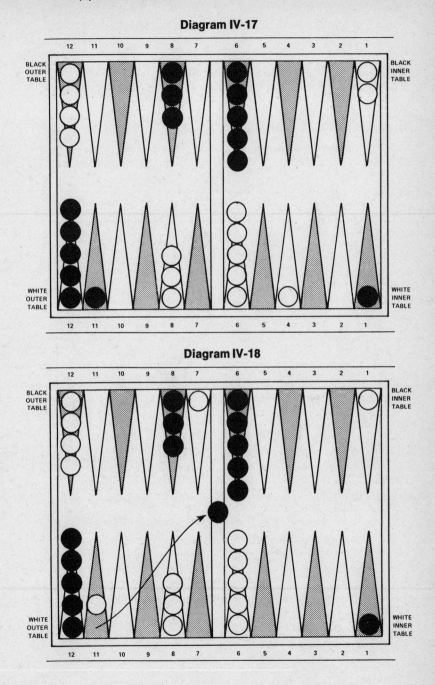

Diagram IV-18

a man from the black one point to the black bar point. See
Diagram IV-13.

If he started with 5-4, 4-3, or 4-1 and exposed a blot on his
nine point, hit that blot with one of your men on the black one
point.

If he started with 5-1 and split his back men bring a man
from the black one point to the black nine point. See Diagram
IV-19.

Diagram IV-19

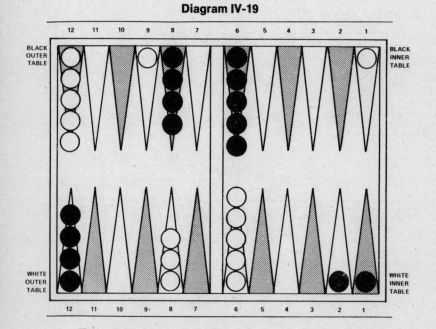

If he started with 3-2 and moved a man to your four point,
hit that man with your 2 and use the 6 to move one of your
back men from the black one point to the black bar point.
See Diagram IV-20.

If he started with 2-1 and made the basic play you are in
trouble. The best of a lot of bad plays is to move to your
eleven point with the 2 and to the black bar point with the 6.
See Diagram IV-21.

Diagram IV-20

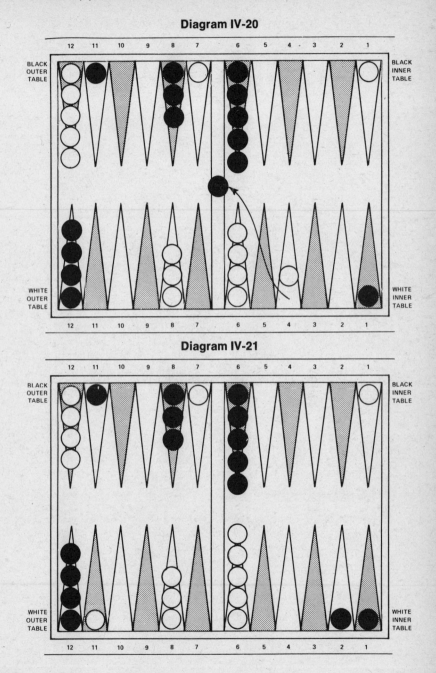

Diagram IV-21

Incidentally, the combination of a Black roll of 2-1 followed by a roll of 6-3 by you is just as bad. Here you should make the same type of play. Move your back man to the black bar point with the 6 and a man from the black twelve point to your ten point with the 3.

6-1   No change.

5-4   Make the basic play unless Black has already exposed a man on his ten point, in which case you hit him with a man from the black one point.

5-3   Make the three point unless:

(a) Black has exposed a man on your ten point, in which case you hit him with the 3 and move a man to your eight point with the 5. See Diagram IV-22.

Diagram IV-22

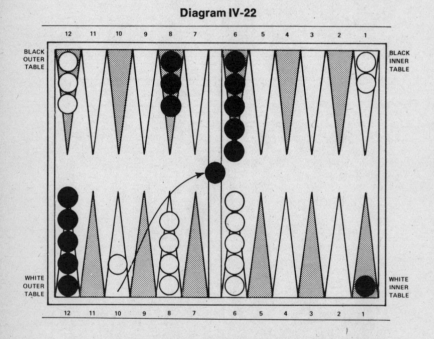

(b) Black has exposed a blot on his nine point, in which case you hit that blot with one of your men on the black one point.

Diagram IV-23

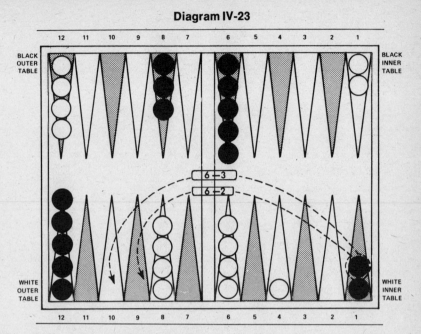

5-2 Unless Black has moved a man from your one point to your nine or ten point, make the basic play. If he has done this, play the 5 normally but use the 2 to expose a blot on your four point. See Diagram IV-23.

5-1 No change.

4-3 If you can hit a blot in your outer table or in the black inner table, do so. If Black has split his back men make the play shown in Diagram IV-24. Here Black has played 5-1, so you use the 4 to move a man from the black twelve point to your nine point and the 3 to move one of your back men from the black one point to the black four point. You don't expose two blots in your outer table because there are too many combination shots which will hit one or the other of them. Otherwise, make the basic play.

4-2 No change unless you can hit a blot worth hitting.

4-1 There is one important exception here. If Black has moved one of his back men to your two point, hit both blots. See Diagram IV-25.

Diagram IV-24

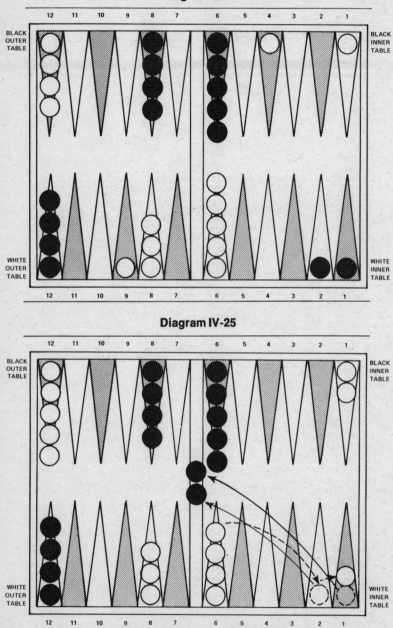

Diagram IV-25

Diagram IV-26

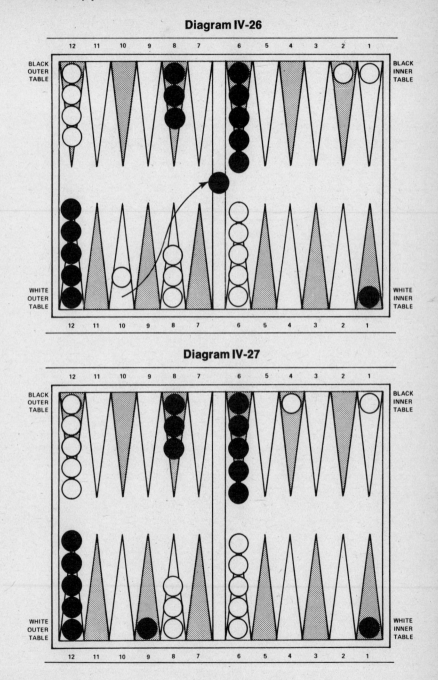

Diagram IV-27

3-2   The same principles apply here as in the case of a 4-3 roll.

3-1   If Black has exposed a man on your ten point use the 3 to hit
        that man with one of your men on the back twelve point and
        use the 1 to split your two back men. See Diagram IV-26.
        Otherwise, just make your five point.

2-1   If Black has exposed a blot on your ten point, use the whole
        roll to hit it with one of the men from the black twelve point.
        If he has exposed a man on your nine point you should move
        a man from the black one point to the black four point. See
        Diagram IV-27. Otherwise, make the basic play.

Lesson V

LET'S PLAY SOME BACKGAMMON THE EARLY GAME

You are now ready to play a little backgammon and to see why you make certain early moves.

Game Number 1

Black starts with 6-5. You reply 3-1; he replies 6-4; and you roll 5-1. The first plays are obvious. Black's second play was to run with his second back man to your eleven point. You had hoped to roll a 2 so as to hit that blot but instead you rolled 5-1 to reach the position shown in Diagram V-1.

It is apparent from this diagram that you used the 5 of your 5-1 to advance a man from the black twelve point to your eight point and the 1 to split your two back men. Why did you make this split?

The reason is that Black has moved a total of twenty-one pips in his first two plays and brought both of his back men out. You have only been able to move ten pips with your two rolls. Not only is Black ahead in a potential running game but he has a fair start toward getting into one. The chances are that he will have to expose a blot in his outer table on one of his next few

Diagram V-1

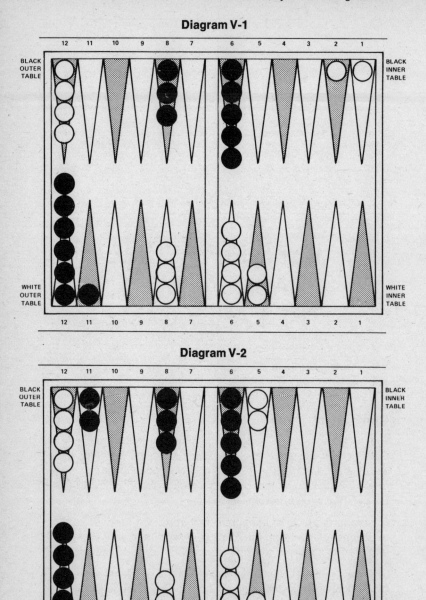

Diagram V-2

rolls. With your back men split you have twice the hitting potential against his outer table. You have exposed two blots but they are on points he really does not want to make this early in the game.

Black rolls 3-2, a nice quiet roll since it enables him to make his eleven point with a man from your twelve point and the blot on your eleven point. You roll 4-3 which is now a very good roll since it enables you to make the black five point and bring up the position shown in Diagram V-2.

Black has the better of the game but you can't help that. He has rolled very well. Your rolls have been inferior but you have made his five point and the two men there will be a thorn in his flesh for a long time.

Black rolls 6-4. This gives him a chance to make his bar point but he doesn't make it because this would leave a blot on his eleven point directly exposed to your men on his five point. Instead Black simply moves a man from your twelve point to his three point. You roll 4-2 and make your four point.

Your game plan is to hit a blot and make Black start a man from the bar. If this happens every extra point you have made will hurt him. If you never hit a blot you will lose the game unless you suddenly start rolling doublets. You are now in the position shown in Diagram V-3.

Black rolls double 4. As we have said, it is hard to play double 4 badly—there are any number of good ways to play this roll. Black decides to move two men from your twelve point to his nine point and two men from his eleven point to his bar point. You roll another 4-2 and move a man from Black's twelve point to your bar point, which brings us to the position shown in Diagram V-4.

Only five plays have been made by each player, but the early game is over. Black has rolled higher numbers, including one large doublet, and is way ahead of you in case a running game develops. His game plan must be to get into a running game; yours to maintain as much contact as possible. In other words, he will want to get those two men off your twelve point into safety in his side of the board; you will want to stay back with your men on his five point and hope to be able to hit a blot with one of them.

Early play is over. We will get back to this game in Lesson VIII.

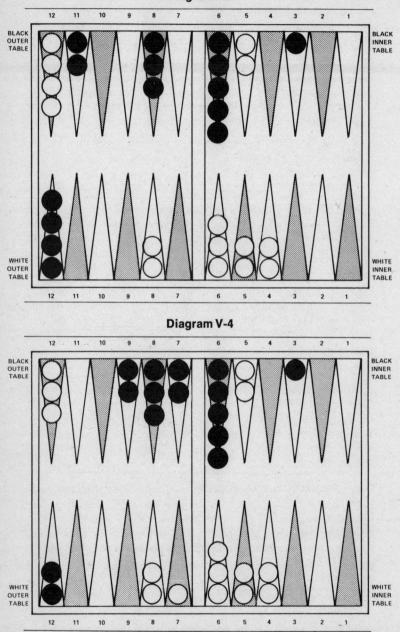

Diagram V-3

Diagram V-4

Game Number 2

You start with 5-2 and make the standard play of one man to
your eight point and one man to your eleven point. Black rolls
6-4 and hits your blot on your eleven point. Your second roll is
5-4. You bring your man in from the bar with the 5 and use the
4 to move one of your back men from the black one point to the
black five point to join the man you just placed there. Black rolls
4-3 and moves the man from your eleven point with the 4 and
one of his men from your twelve point with the 3 to produce the
position shown in Diagram V-5.

Diagram V-5

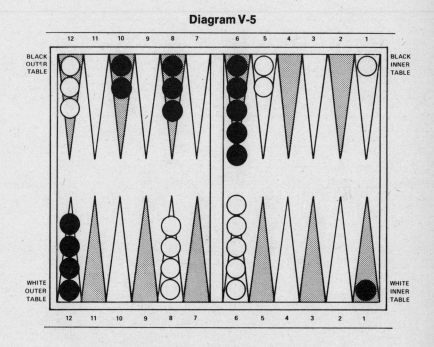

You have lost ground, since one of your men has been sent back
fourteen pips from your eleven point to the bar but you have a
sound defensive position.

You roll 3-1 and make your five point. Black rolls 5-4 and can't
do anything at all good with it. His back man can't move because
you have blocked off a move of either a 4 or a 5. He does the best
he can and moves a man from your twelve point to his four point.

Diagram V-6

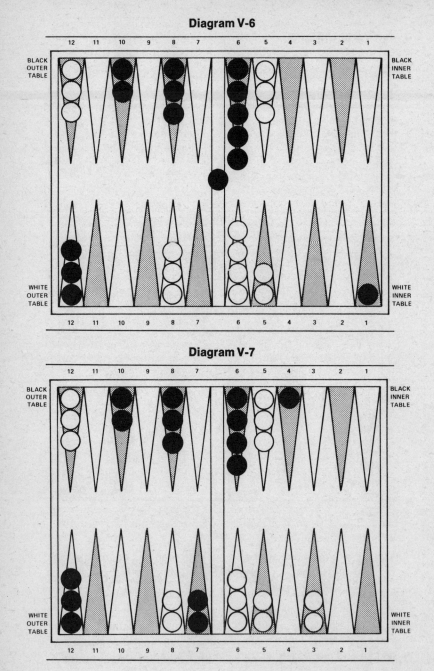

Diagram V-7

You roll another 3-1 and use the 3 to hit his blot on the four point and the 1 to continue on with the same man to leave you with three men on the black five point and no blots anywhere on the board. See Diagram V-6.

You have made up lost ground in case you get into a running game and also have the better position, since you hold both five points.

Black rolls 4-2. He brings the man on the bar in on your four point with the 4 and moves a man to his own four point with the 2. This last blot means nothing right now, since you have nothing that will hit it.

You roll 5-3 and make your three point. Black rolls 6-3 and finds a nice way to play this normally poor roll. He makes your bar point to produce the position shown in Diagram V-7.

Your backgammon player's eye tells you that the running game position is about even. An accurate pip count (see Appendix A) makes your total 149 and Black's total 147, but it is your roll. Furthermore you are a long way from getting into a running game.

Your immediate aim should be to get Black to expose a blot and to hit that blot. Black's immediate aim should be to make some more points in his inner table and then hope to hit a blot in the event that you expose one.

You roll 6-3. You could play safe by moving a man from the black twelve point to your four point but you should not do this. You don't need to play safe right now: Black holds only one point in his inner table. Instead you move a man from the black five point to your eleven point. Black can hit this man with any 4, 3-1 or double 2.

Will he? Not if he knows what he is doing—unless he is lucky enough to roll double 4. He has an even game if he plays safe. He is likely to lose immediately if he gambles.

Black does roll 4-3. He looks longingly at your blot but then proceeds to move a man from his eight point to join his blot on his four point with the 4 and a man around the corner to his own ten point with the 3.

You roll a 6-1 and move your blot all the way to your four point. You exposed him for one roll; there is no need to leave him exposed. Black rolls 6-4 and uses the 6 to move a man from the ten point to his own four point and the 4 to move a man from his six point to his two point.

You roll double 6 and move the two men from the black five point to your eight point. Black rolls 3-1 and makes his five point to produce the position shown in Diagram V-8.

Diagram V-8

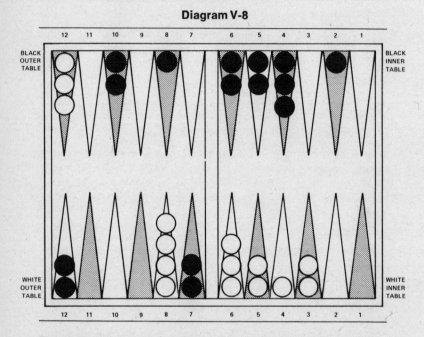

The early play is over since your whole plan is to get into a running game; Black's is to maintain contact in the hope of hitting a blot. We will return to this game in Lesson VIII.

Game Number 3

You start with 6-4 and bring a back man from the black one point to the black eleven point. Black replies with double 2. He uses two of the 2's to hit your blot on the eleven point and the other two to make his four point. You roll 5-1.

You have two ways to play this roll. Both are bad. One way is to use the 5 to bring your man in from the bar and the 1 to move the other man in the black inner table to the black two point. This produces the position shown in Diagram V-9. The other way is to use the 1 to bring your man in from the bar and the 5 to move

Diagram V-9

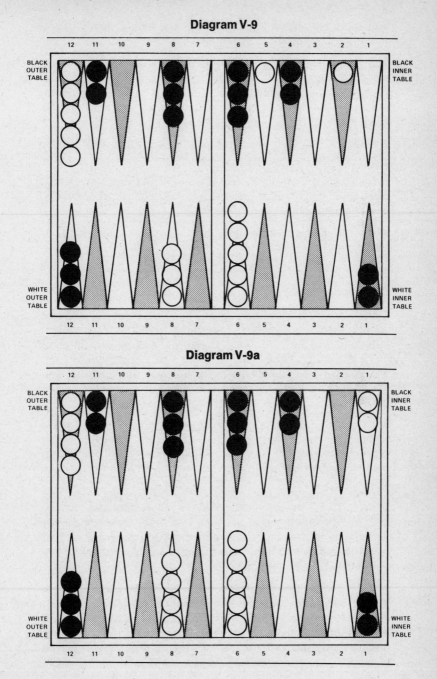

Diagram V-9a

a man from the black twelve point to your eight point. This produces the position shown in Diagram V-9a.

The first play is an effort to get right back into the game. Black will hit the man on his five point if he can. If he can point on him the game will probably end quickly. If he doesn't point on him you will have a chance to equalize matters by making his five point.

The second play insures you a bad game but will probably allow you to struggle on and possibly get back into the contest.

Black rolls 3-1 and you roll 5-4. Diagram V-10 shows what would have happened if you had elected the first play. Diagram V-10a, if you had made the second one.

We will come back to position 10 in Lesson VII and to 10a in Lesson VIII.

Game Number 4

You start with 3-1 and make your five point. Black rolls double 6 and makes both bar points. You roll 4-1. You can play safe by moving a man from the black twelve point to your eight point but this would be poor tactics. Black has jumped out in front and you want to complicate the position, if you can. So, you use the 1 to move a back man forward in Black's inner table and the 4 to expose a blot in your outer board.

You have no objection to Black hitting this blot. You can afford to start that man over again. In addition, if he does hit him he will probably leave you some come-back shots and it will be greatly to your advantage to thus get a blot-hitting contest started.

Black rolls 5-4 and is immediately in mild trouble. He has to give you a shot no matter how he plays these numbers. Finally he decides to move the two men from your bar point to your twelve and eleven points. This exposes his blot to any 2. See Diagram V-11.

You roll 5-4 and make your four point. Black rolls 6-3 and again has to leave a blot somewhere. He elects to use the 6 to move a man from your twelve point to his bar point and the 3 to move the blot on your eleven point forward to his own eleven point. It is only exposed to 6-4 and 6-3 so that is the best he can do.

Diagram V-10

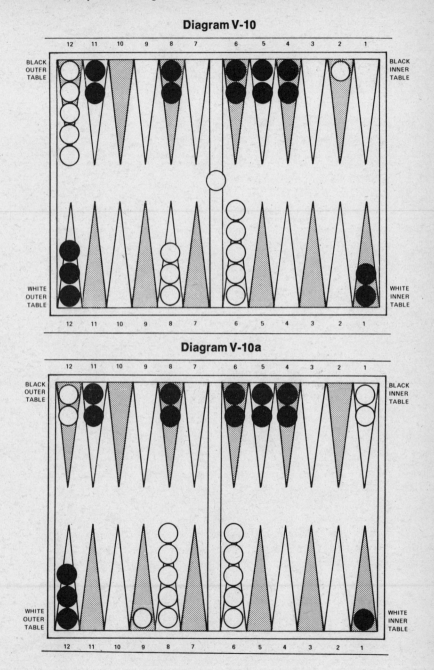

Diagram V-10a

Diagram V-11

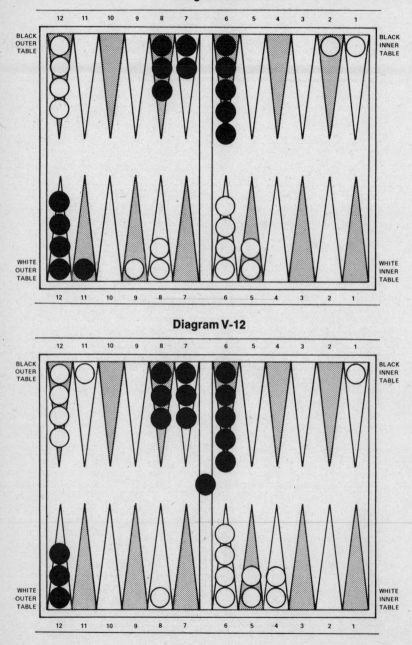

Diagram V-12

You roll 6-3 and proceed to hit that blot with your man on the black two point. He rolls 5-4 and can't come in. The position is now as shown in Diagram V-12.

You have a slight advantage but you are not ready to double as yet (more on doubles in Lesson VII). You roll 5-1 and consider your play. You decide to move the blot on the black eleven point over to your nine point with the 5 and a man from your six point to your five point with the 1. Why didn't you simply make your eight point instead of voluntarily leaving two blots? Because your two blots are only exposed to 6-3, 6-2, and 5-3 and if Black doesn't hit one of them you are in an excellent position to make another point in your board and to really hamper the movement of that man now on your bar.

Black rolls a 5-2. He has to come in with the 2 and he uses the 5 to hit your blot on his one point. See the position in Diagram V-13.

Isn't this a poor play—to move down to his one point this early in the game and to be leaving a blot at the same time? It is a poor play but it is his last gasp. If he simply moved a man from your twelve point to his eight point you would probably point on that man on your two point. This play will keep you busy since

Diagram V-13

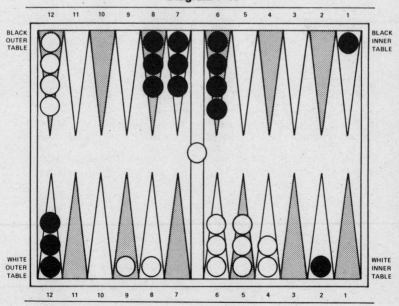

Diagram V-14

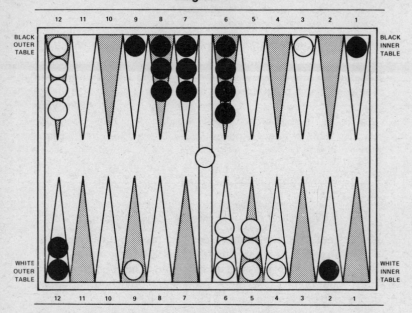

you will have to use part of your roll to bring your man in from the bar.

You roll 6-3 and have to use the 3 to bring your man in from the bar and your best play with the 6 is to hit the blot on your two point. If Black hadn't hit you on his one point at his last turn to play you would have been able to make that two point.

Black rolls 4-2. He hits your blot on your two point with the 2 and moves a man to his nine point with the 4. This produces the position shown in Diagram V-14, which we will come back to in Lesson VIII.

Lesson VI

THE ARITHMETIC OF BACKGAMMON

Let's look at an apparently simple backgammon position. See Diagram VI-1. You are in mighty good shape—your opponent has a man on the bar and you are bearing off.

Diagram VI-1

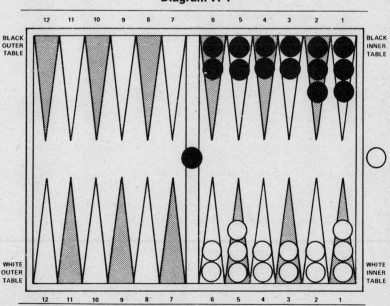

Then trouble rears its ugly head. You roll double 5. You have a choice between bearing off three men and moving one man from your six point to your one point or bearing two men off and moving both men from your six point to your one point. In either case you must leave a blot. Which play do you make?

Is that extra man off going to make any difference in the final result of the game? Possibly, one time in several hundred! For all practical purposes you are going to win if your blot survives and lose if he is hit. It's as simple as that!

Hunch players gaze at the stars and ask, "Will my opponent throw a 6, or will he throw a 5?" Then they mentally toss a coin and make their play. Backgammon players don't waste time on the stars or on hunches. They leave the blot on the five point because in that position he can only be hit with any 5. On the other hand, a blot on the six point can be hit, not only with any 6, **but with a 5-1!**

We'll come back to this position in a little while and tell you just how much better the right play is. Meanwhile we want to develop a few tables to show you how to figure all one-roll and some two-roll problems.

There are six faces on a die. Hence there are six possible results when one die is thrown and six times six, or thirty-six, possible results when two dice are rolled. Table 1 shows these thirty-six possibilities.

TABLE 1

Rolls Possible with Two Dice

1-1	1-2	1-3	1-4	1-5	1-6
2-1	2-2	2-3	2-4	2-5	2-6
3-1	3-2	3-3	3-4	3-5	3-6
4-1	4-2	4-3	4-4	4-5	4-6
5-1	5-2	5-3	5-4	5-5	5-6
6-1	6-2	6-3	6-4	6-5	6-6

While you can work out all one-roll probabilities from this table, all that we want you to learn right now is:

(a) There are exactly 36 rolls with two dice.
(b) There is just one way to roll a specific doublet—hence the chance of rolling a 4-4 is 1 in 36.

(c) There are two ways to roll any ordinary number—hence the chance of rolling a 5-3 is 2 in 36.

(d) There are eleven ways for a specified number to be rolled—hence the chance of rolling a 3 is 11 in 36.

Table 2 is derived from Table 1.

TABLE 2

Number of open points	Number of rolls which will allow you to bring in from the bar	
	One man	Two men
1	11	1
2	20	4
3	27	9
4	32	16
5	35	25

Once you know that the number 11 represents the number of rolls that will include a specific number on at least one die you can derive the rest of column two by adding 9 for a second open point; 7 for a third one; 5 for the fourth; 3 for the fifth; and finally one more to give a total of 36 ways to enter an open board.

Why do you start by adding 9 to 11? Aren't there 11 ways to roll any number? Of course there are, but you can count any given roll only once. Suppose the open points are 3 and 1. Your 11 ways to roll a 3 include 3-1 and 1-3—and so do your 11 ways to roll a 1. You can't count them twice, so you just add 9 more for your second open point. Similarly, when you have a third open point—say the 5—you just add 7 because you have already counted 5-3, 3-5, 5-1, and 1-5.

In order to derive column three, just note that when you have to bring in two men the number of successful rolls is the square of the number of open points—$1 \times 1 = 1$ with one point open; $2 \times 2 = 4$ with two points open; et cetera.

Blots are like death and taxes. They can't be avoided. A game without a blot occurs once in a blue moon. When your opponent has closed (that is, he has two or more men on a point) only one or two points in his inner table, you expect to bring a hit blot right back in. It doesn't always happen—everyone has some bad luck. Anyway, in the early game if you do expose a blot you want to expose it where it will do some good if it is not hit. Later on, when a hit blot may well mean the loss of the game you will want to know the exact chances that it will be hit. This probability will, of course, vary with the distance between the blot and the opponent's man threatening him. See Table 3.

TABLE 3

Distance between blot and threat	Rolls which can hit blot with		Total number of ways to hit blot
	single die	combination of both dice	
24		Double 6	1
20 or 15		Double 5	1
16		Double 4	1
12		Double 6, 4, and 3	3
11		6-5	2
10		6-4, double 5	3
9		6-3, 5-4, double 3	5
8		6-2, 5-3, double 4 and 2	6
7		6-1, 5-2, 4-3	6
6	Any 6	5-1, 4-2, double 3 and 2	17
5	Any 5	4-1, 3-2	15
4	Any 4	3-1, double 2 and 1	15
3	Any 3	2-1, double 1	14
2	Any 2	Double 1	12
1	Any 1		11

Columns two and three show the actual rolls which will hit your blot for each of the possible distances. Column four gives the total number of ways that your blot can be hit.

Get into the habit of counting the actual rolls which will hit you whenever that knowledge is important. Most of the time these simple rules will suffice:

1. Any indirect shot (distance 7 or more) is better than any direct shot (distance 6 or less).
2. If you expose to a direct shot, the *closer* the better. The number of ways that you can be hit will vary from 11 to 17.
3. If you expose to an indirect shot, the *further away* the better. The number of ways you can be hit will vary from 6 to 1.

At times it is convenient to refer to points which are under the control of one of the two players (that is, they are occupied by more than one man) as blocks—they prevent, or block, the use of that point by the other player.

It is important to note that Table 3 is based upon the assumption that there are no intervening blocks which impede the attacker's progress. Since the number of ways a blot can be hit depends not only upon the distance between the threat and the blot, but also upon the number of intervening blocks and upon their location, it is not practical to cover every possibility. This complication will not bother you in the least provided you get into the habit of counting the number of ways a blot can be hit. All you need to remember is that there is just one way to roll a doublet, two ways to roll any ordinary number, and eleven ways to roll any specific number with a single die.

Now let us go back to Diagram VI-1 and your roll of double 5. If you expose a blot on your five point it can only be hit by a direct 5—eleven different ways. Your men on the one, two, three, and four points have blocked out all combination shots. If you expose your blot on the six point it is open to a hit by any direct 6 (eleven different ways) and also to a 5-1 combination roll—that is, to a total count of thirteen different ways. Note that your blocks on the one, two, three, and four points have eliminated all other combinations.

On the average you are going to lose eleven games out of thirty-six when you leave your blot on the five point and thirteen games out of thirty-six when you leave your blot on the six point. Why lose an extra two games in thirty-six?

Now let's look at Diagrams IV-11 and IV-12, reproduced here as Diagrams VI-2 and VI-3. In Diagram VI-2 your blot is exposed to twelve different rolls—any 1 by one of the men on your twelve point and double 4 by one of his back men on your one point. Note that your men on your bar point block the back men from hitting him with a double 6 or double 3.

In Diagram VI-3 the blot on your eight point is exposed only to 5-2 and 4-3 (four different rolls). Here your men on the two and bar points prevent him from hitting your blot with a 6-1. Twelve ways are a lot more than four, but there are two considerations which make the play shown in Diagram VI-2 preferable. One is that it won't be a tragedy if your blot is hit in this position. The other, and really your primary consideration at the moment, is that the overall position with three points made in a row (Diagram VI-2) is far superior to your position in Diagram VI-3.

Here is a rather unusual position. See Diagram VI-4. Your last roll was 6-5 which you used to move a man from the black ten point to your four point. Black then rolled 3-2 and could not hit your blot. You proceed to roll 4-1. You are not happy about this

Diagram VI-2

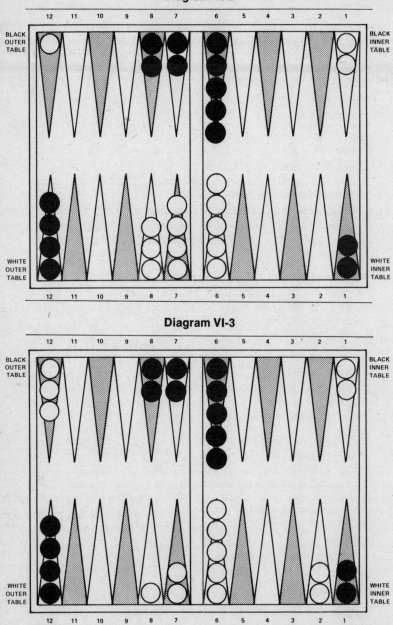

Diagram VI-3

Diagram VI-4

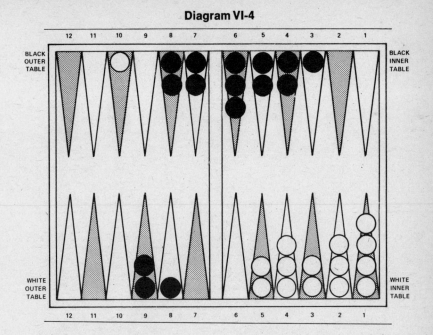

roll. You should not really be surprised that you were not able to pass Black's men. There were sixteen different rolls which would have left you in difficulty (5-1, 4-2, 4-1, 3-2, 3-1, 2-1, double 6, double 3, double 2, double 1). Your first thought is to leave that man on the black ten point where he is and move up in your inner table, but you decide to make an accurate count. There are seventeen different ways one of the men on your nine point can hit him (the eleven 6's plus 5-1, 4-2, double 3, and double 2). In addition the man on your eight point can hit you with 5-2 or 4-3. Thus, if you leave your blot where it is, it will be exposed to twenty-one shots.

Now suppose you move him right up to your ten point. He is now exposed to a direct shot by any 1 or any 2. There are twenty different ways of throwing one of two specific numbers (11 + 9). So, you find that your man is in slightly less danger close-up than well back. An advanced player would not have bothered with all this computation. He would see that if he brought the man forward, and the blot was not hit, he would almost surely win the game; if he left him back on the black ten point, and he lived, there would still remain the problem of getting him past Black's sentinels.

Diagram VI-5

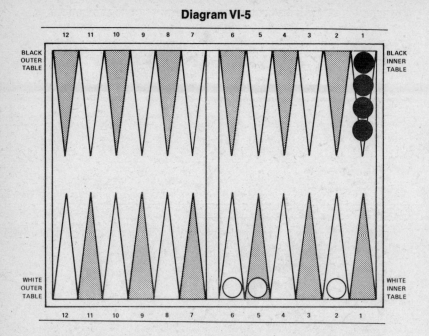

Let's take a look at a typical end game situation. See Diagram VI-5. You roll 3-2. Obviously, you use the 2 to bear off the man on the two point. How do you play the 3? Do you leave the remaining two men on the six and the two points or on the five and the three points? Does it make any difference? It won't if Black ends the game on his next roll by throwing a doublet!

Otherwise, it will! If you have your men on the six and two points you will get them off on your next roll with any 6 except 6-1 (nine different rolls) and with any double 5, 4, 3, or 2 (four more rolls) for a total of thirteen different rolls.

If you have your men on the five and three points you will get them both off with any 6 except 6-1 and 6-2 (seven different rolls), plus any 5 except 5-1 and 5-2 (five additional rolls, not seven, because you have already counted 6-5 among your 6's), plus double 4 or 3 (two more rolls) for a total of fourteen different rolls. Not much difference you say! Isn't it worthwhile to win one more game out of thirty-six when it costs you nothing?

Similar calculations can be made for each of the possible end game positions where you have only one or two men left to bear off. The first three columns of Table 4 show the results of such calculations. The fourth column gives your probability ("chance" or "likelihood" if you prefer either of these terms) of winning. Any time you know the number of rolls favorable to a given event all that you need to do to get the probability of its occurring is to divide by the number of possible ways, thirty-six, and multiply by 100 to convert it to a percentage. The last column is the result of further calculations involving two rolls.

You should learn to work out the figures in column three on your own. After a little practice this will become fairly easy and, therefore, there is no need to memorize it.

In instances where you can't end the game but will be down to one or two men after completing your play you will usually be able to choose how to leave your men. In this connection the

TABLE 4

Probability of Bearing Off the Last One or Two Men in One or Two Rolls

Total points to go	Points on which your man or men are located	In one roll you have the following		In two rolls you have the following probability of winning (percent)
		Number of winning rolls	Probability of winning (percent)	
2	2	36	100	100
	Both on 1	36	100	100
3	3	36	100	100
	2 and 1	36	100	100
4	4	34	94	100
	3 and 1	34	94	100
	Both on 2	26	72	100
5	5	31	86	100
	4 and 1	29	81	100
	3 and 2	25	69	100
6	6	27	75	100
	5 and 1	23	64	100
	4 and 2	23	64	100
	Both on 3	17	47	100
7	5 and 2	19	53	99+
	4 and 3	17	47	99+
	6 and 1	15	42	99+
8	5 and 3	14	39	99
	6 and 2	13	36	99
	Both on 4	11	31	98
9	5 and 4	10	28	96
	6 and 3	10	28	97
10	6 and 4	8	22	93
	Both on 5	6	17	92
11	6 and 5	6	17	88
12	Both on 6	4	11	78

following short series of rules will solve all of your problems quickly:

(a) *Whenever possible, always leave only one man.*

(b) When you must leave two men never leave them on the same point; place the man that will be farther away on the five point (first choice), four point (second choice), or six point (third choice).

As for column five just note that you are an overwhelming favorite to get two men off in two rolls no matter how far back they are placed in your board.

Lesson VII

DOUBLES AND REDOUBLES

It is now necessary to discuss the doubling cube mentioned in Lesson I. Physically the doubling cube is an overgrown die with the numbers 2, 4, 8, 16, 32, and 64 on its six faces.

Backgammon was played for thousands of years without the doubling cube. Then, sometime in the twenties, an unsung, unremembered genius began using it and thus transformed a rather uninteresting game into one of the most fascinating games there is.

Whether you play for money, marbles, or chalk, the doubling feature speeds up and enlivens the game. Once the value of a single unit is agreed upon, the first double raises the "count" (the number of units you are playing for at the moment) from 1 to 2; the next double will raise the count from 2 to 4; the next, from 4 to 8; and so on. Doubles are made in two ways:

(a) *Automatically:* Each tie in the opening throw doubles the previous count. Automatic doubles are not played in tournaments and, if you agree to play them, be sure you limit their number. Beware of the man who wants to play unlimited automatic doubles. Remember that four doubles increase the count from one to sixteen and not from one to four.

(b) *Voluntarily:* Either player may make the first voluntary (or optional) double. After that the right to double the previous count (that is, to redouble) alternates, being always with the man who accepted the previous double.

A double, or redouble, may be offered only when it is the player's turn to play and before he has thrown the dice. It may be accepted or it may be declined. A refusal terminates the game and the refusing player loses whatever the count was before the double was offered.

At the start of the game the doubling cube is placed alongside the board, approximately halfway between the two sides, with the number 32 or 64 up. (The cube is then turned to 2 if there is an automatic double, to 4 if there are two automatic doubles, etc.)

When a player wants to offer the first voluntary double he says, "Double," and, turning the doubling cube to the next higher number (that is, from 64 to 2, 2 to 4, etc.), moves it toward his opponent.

If the opponent accepts the double he moves the cube to his side of the board. If he refuses the double the game is over.

Redoubles are made in a similar manner.

When the doubling cube is on your side of the board you are said to "own the cube." Possession of the cube is a very real advantage. You are the only one who can redouble—the count cannot be further increased unless you desire it!

It is very important to realize that there are positions which warrant a first voluntary double (this moves the cube from the center of the table to your opponent's side) but which do not warrant a redouble (this moves the cube from your side of the table to your opponent's).

Doubling situations fall naturally into one of four main classes:

1. *Positional doubles,* those doubles based upon the fact that your position is sounder than your opponent's.
2. *Running game doubles,* those doubles based upon the fact that you are in a running game (or near running game) and your men are further advanced than your opponent's men.
3. *General doubles,* those doubles based upon a combination of the preceding two classes.
4. *End game doubles,* those doubles based upon your position, relative to that of your opponent, in the last stages of bearing off.

When should you double? Anytime you feel that, if you were to get to the same position a thousand times, you would win more points by doubling than by playing on.

When should you accept a correct double? Any time you feel that, if you were doubled a thousand times in the same position, your net loss if you accepted all of the doubles would be less than if you refused them.

When should you refuse a double? When you expect to lose more by accepting than by refusing.

Your experience is the only thing that can help you with doubles in Classes 1 and 3. For doubles in Class 2 we are going to give you a rather simple rule of thumb (providing you are willing to make an accurate pip count of both your own position and that of your opponent) which will place you immediately in the expert class as far as these doubles are concerned.

It will be work to learn how to make these pip counts but, if you have not already done so, we strongly recommend that you turn to Appendix A and take time to learn how to count the positions. This ability will repay you many times over for the effort expended in learning.

In a running game situation when you are ahead—should you double? When you are behind—should you refuse a double if Black offers one? If you have learned to make a pip count of your own and your opponent's position, you can work out the difference in the two counts and, with this information, determine the doubling number. This doubling number will answer both of these questions for you.

The doubling number is determined by dividing the lower of the two total pip counts by the difference in the two counts. You do not have to work this out to three decimals, or even to one decimal—all you need to know is what two natural numbers (what two integers) it lies between. Suppose your pip count is 106 and that Black's pip count is 120. Your lead is 14 pips. The

TABLE 5
Doubling Number
Range in which you double, redouble, or refuse a double

	Always	Sometimes	Never
Double	**Under 8**	**8 to 10**	**Over 10**
Redouble	**Under 6**	**6 to 8**	**Over 8**
Refuse a double	**Under 5**	**5 to 6**	**Over 6**

doubling number is 106 divided by 14. It is more than 7 and less than 8.

Once you know the doubling number all that you need to do is to look at the preceding table and act in accordance with it! In the example just given your doubling number was between 7 and 8. Table 5 shows that you should offer the first double since you always do this when the doubling number is less than 8.

How about offering a redouble? The range for consideration is 6 to 8 and, since you are closer to 8 than to 6, you probably won't redouble. Then why do you consider it at all? Because you may know that your opponent is a pessimist in running game situations and is likely to refuse the double. If you expect him to accept, wait a roll or two—thus keeping the cube on your side for the moment.

If you want to try to approximate by means of the backgammon player's eye and your general experience, you can do so; if you really want to know how to handle running game doubles, learn how to make pip counts and to use the doubling number.

Diagram VII-1

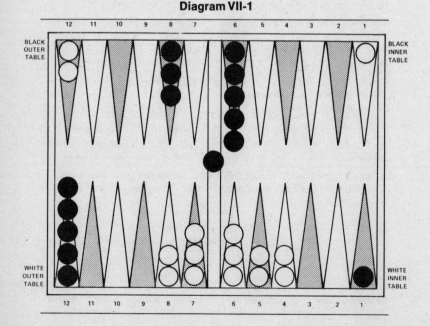

Diagram VII-2

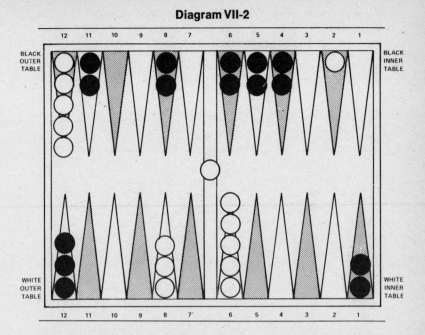

Class 1 (Positional) doubles usually represent early game problems and are complicated by gammon possibilities. Thus, a position may be so strong that you don't want to double because you know that your opponent will refuse. Diagram VII-1 shows one such position.

You don't need any experience at all to see that the worst that can happen to you in this position is that you make a poor roll and Black replies with 3-2 to make the three point in your inner table. In that case you can still double and Black will still refuse. On the other hand, if you have just a little more good luck you will be gammoning him.

Don't double—just roll!

Diagram VII-2 repeats Diagram V-10. You have just failed to bring a man in from the bar and Black doubles you. Was he right to double you? Yes, he was. His position is very strong, yours is bad. Then why doesn't he play on for a gammon? Because he has only three rolls that will crush you. They are double 6, double 4, and double 3. If he doesn't get one of them and you roll any 2, or 3-1, or double 1, your position will be good enough for you to take a double. Right now it isn't that good and you refuse.

We will discuss Class 3 doubles in the next lesson where we carry forward the games we started in Lesson IV. Class 4 doubles will be discussed in Lesson X.

Lesson VIII

LET'S PLAY SOME MORE BACKGAMMON (THE MIDDLE GAME)

Just when does the middle game begin and end? There is no formula for this in backgammon any more than there is in chess, but for purposes of this book it will begin:

(a) When the position is such that a hit blot is likely to determine the result of the game, or

(b) When the first double is accepted.

It will end:

(a) When a running game position is reached, or

(b) When the first man is borne off, or

(c) When one player closes his board (has made all six points in his inner table) against an adverse man, or men, on the bar.

It is entirely possible to go from the early game directly into a running game. In Lesson II we discussed a game in which the first two rolls of each player were 6-5 and each player moved his back men from his opponent's one point to his opponent's twelve point. After only four rolls (two by each player) they were in a running game situation—the early game was over and the middle game had never existed!

Diagram VIII-1

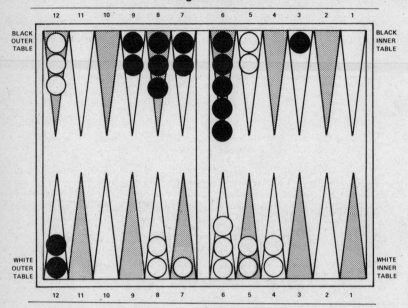

In Diagram V-4 (repeated here for convenience as Diagram VIII-1) we return to Game Number 1 where each player has made only five moves. Yet the whole game plan has been determined and we are in a middle game situation.

It is Black's roll, but instead of rolling he doubles. Is it correct to do this? Should you accept?

Black clearly has an advantage since he has outrolled you considerably. His position is sound and his only real problem is to get his two men on your twelve point safely across to his side of the table.

Your position is also sound: your men on his five point are a potential threat against his men that must pass them. You are not fully in a running game but the position should be counted.

A quick use of the backgammon player's eye shows that, if the two white men on the black five point were advanced twelve points each to the white eight point, the game would be almost exactly even. In other words, if you as White could be given an extra double 6, it would be an even game.

If you have followed our advice in Lesson VII and learned how to make a pip count you will see that Black's count is 115 and your count 138 (with a difference of 23 pips), so that the doubling number is 115/23 or exactly 5.

Hence, if it were just a running game situation you should refuse the double, but the slight chance that you can hit a blot and turn the game around makes it a proper take and you accept.

Black's next roll is 6-4 and you wish you had given up. He has moved those two men on your twelve point to a safe position in his outer table and also has rolled an above average number. You come back with 6-5 and use the 6 to move a man from the black twelve point to your own bar point and the 5 to move a man from your eight point to your three point. You have gained one pip and are now only twenty-two pips behind but your position was worsened materially.

Block now rolls 3-2 and moves two men to his six point (one man from his nine point and one man from his eight point). You roll double 6 and all of a sudden things look brighter. You

Diagram VIII-2

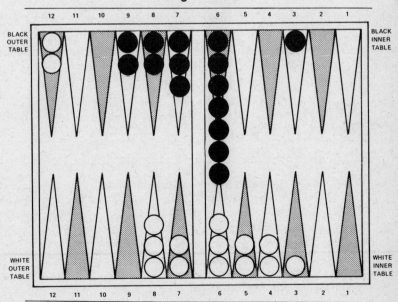

will be only three pips behind after you play this double 6 and you decide to move your two back men from the black five point to your own eight point to produce the position shown in Diagram VIII-2.

Why is this the proper play for you to make when you will still be behind in the running game? Because those two men on the black five point would have become a liability if left there. It is better to get out and hope to pick up those three pips in the next few rolls. You are now in a running game, which we will get back to in Lesson IX.

Diagram VIII-3

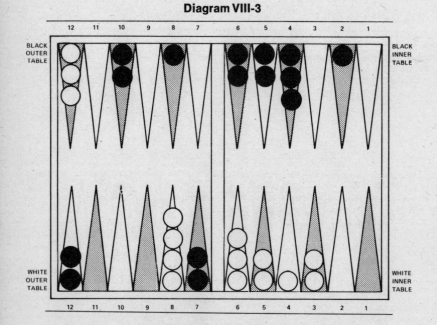

In Diagram V-8 (repeated here for convenience as Diagram VIII-3) we return to Game Number 2. It is your roll and your backgammon player's eye tells you that you have an advantage, so there is no need to make a pip count. You are not going to double because, while you will want to get into a running game and will do your best to do so, there are plenty of problems ahead. You may be lucky and never leave a blot, but the odds are that you will have to leave one.

You roll 5-4 and move a man from the black twelve point to your four point. Black rolls 3-2 and moves a man from his ten point to his five point. You roll 6-5 and move a man from your eight point to your two point with the 6 and use the 5 to move a man from your six point to your one point. Black rolls 4-3 and moves a man from his ten point to his three point to bring up the position shown in Diagram VIII-4.

Why did you use the 5 in your last roll to move a man from your six point to your one point when you could have moved a man from your eight point to your three point?

Because your game plan in this position is to keep from giving Black a shot. You want to keep as many men outside your inner table as possible so as to allow you to play 6's safely.

Diagram VIII-4

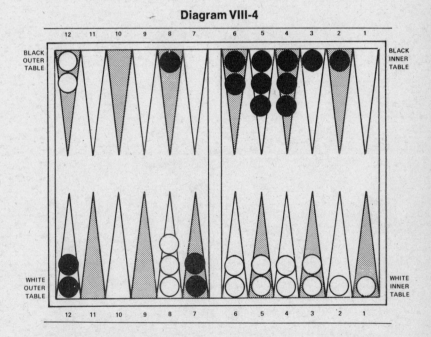

It is evident that you lead by a country mile in the potential running game and some players might even double at this point, on the theory that there is a chance not to leave a blot and that, even if one is left, the odds are that it will not be hit.

Diagram VIII-5

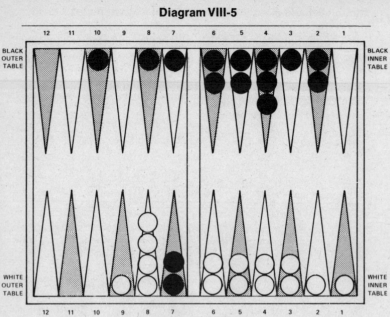

Diagram VIII-6

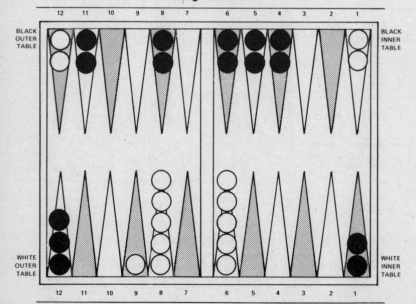

Of course, Black would take a double if it were offered.

You don't double and proceed to roll 5-4. Our recommendation here is that you have the tooth out immediately. Move the two men on the black twelve point forward to your eight and nine points.

The odds are 25 to 11 that Black won't hit your blot and, if he misses, you will be able to double immediately. If he misses with double 4, 5, or 6, he will have a proper take of your double; otherwise, the game is over.

Furthermore, unless he hits you with double 2 (which will allow him to cover his blots on his two and three points) you will have plenty of return action going for you. Black rolls double 3 and moves the men on your twelve point to his bar point and ten point with three of the 3's and uses the fourth 3 to move a man from his five point to his two point, thus producing the position shown in Diagram VIII-5.

We now return to Game Number 3. Diagram V-10a is reproduced here as Diagram VIII-6. Black doubles and you decide to accept. Not that this acceptance is recommended: your position is very

Diagram VIII-7

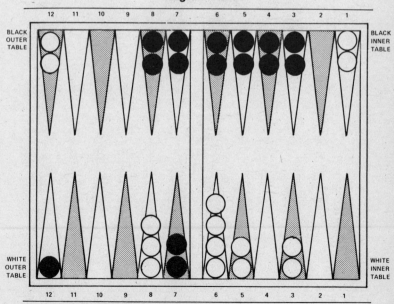

unsound, but you do hold his one point and hope springs eternal in the human breast.

Black rolls 6-3 and moves the men from his eleven point to his eight and five points. You roll 6-5 and decide to use this roll to make your three point with the blot on your nine point and one of the men on your eight point. Black rolls double 6 and makes both bar points. He doesn't worry about leaving a blot on your twelve point. He has your two back men on his one point practically blocked and anticipates no trouble if his blot is hit.

You roll 3-1 and should not bother with his blot at all. Just make your five point. Black rolls 5-2 and completes his prime (makes six points in a row) by moving two men to his three point from his eight and five points. See Diagram VIII-7 (the same position shown as Diagram X-1, Lesson X).

Now back to Game Number 4. Diagram V-14 is reproduced as Diagram VIII-8. Black has been kept alive, but still is in a bad position. Your only bad roll is double 6, which you won't be able

Diagram VIII-8

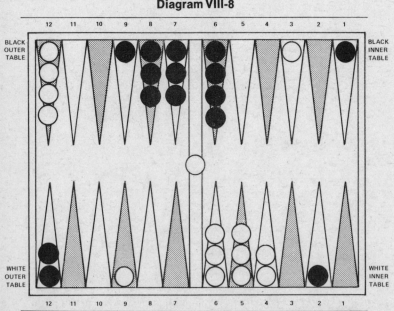

to play at all on account of your man on the bar. There are quite a few crushing rolls and you think about doubling but decide not to on the theory that it rarely pays to double when you have a man on the bar.

You roll double 4. This is not one of your best rolls but it plays nicely. You bring your man in from the bar; move two men from the black twelve point to your nine point and hit his blot on your two point with your last 4. Black rolls 6-3; brings his man on the bar to your three point with the 3 and hits your blot on his three point with the 6. See Diagram VIII-9. You are back on the

Diagram VIII-9

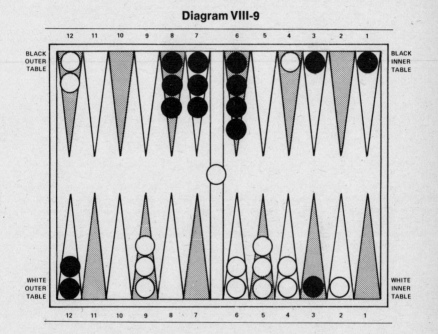

bar, but Black has two blots exposed in his home board. You decide to double him. Black really should not accept, but he sees that if you miss his blots in his inner table and he can get that man on your three point to safety, he will be well ahead in the running game—so he accepts.

He sure wishes he hadn't because you proceed to roll double 3. You hit his blot on his three point as you enter your man from the bar with the first 3; cover your blot on your two point with the second 3; hit his blot on your three point with the last two 3's. Black rolls 4-2 and can't bring either man in from the bar. We will return to this game in Lesson X. See Diagram X-6.

Lesson IX

FINISHING THE
RUNNING GAME

In Lesson II we discussed a game where both players rolled 6-5 on their first two rolls to arrive at the position shown in Diagram II-2 (repeated as Diagram IX-1) as an example of how it was possible for the early game to be extremely short and the middle game nonexistent. In continuing this game now we shall see how to play a long running game. It is your move and that gives you a slight edge. Your game plan and Black's will be the same. You will want to get your men into your home table as quickly as possible. At the same time, while you won't want to bring them all onto the six point, you won't want to waste too much time in getting them in. Accordingly, you will bring men to the five and four points but not try for the lower-numbered points. Black will be using the same tactics and neither of you will consider doubling for a while unless one of you really outrolls his opponent.

Your first three rolls in order are 5-2, 4-3, and 6-2. Black's are 6-1, 4-2, and double 3.

You bring two men around the corner with each of your first two rolls; on the third roll you can not repeat this procedure because this will leave you with a blot on the black twelve point. Your 6 is easy. You move a man from the black twelve point to your bar point. The 2 is also easy. You continue with that same man to your five point.

Diagram IX-1

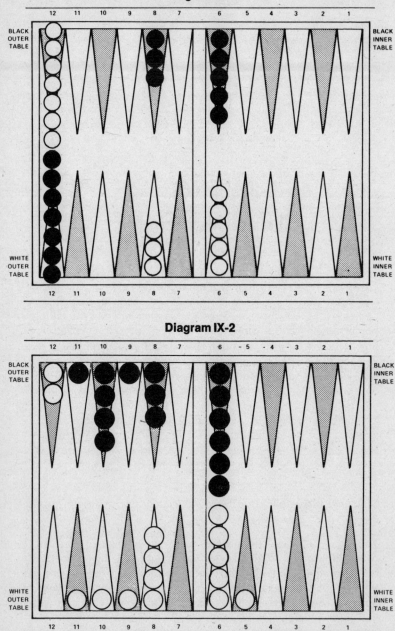

Diagram IX-2

Black plays his 6-1 by moving a man from your twelve point to his six point. He brings two men around from your twelve point with the 4-2 and clears it with double 3, to bring about the position shown in Diagram IX-2. There is no need to make a pip count here but there is a little trick of the trade to tell you exactly how you stand. Three rolls back you were even. Both of your first rolls were 7's. Still even. You gained one pip on the next roll. 7 against 6. You lost four pips the next roll—12 for Black against 8 for you—so Black is now three pips ahead.

You roll 5-3. You could bring your last two men around the corner, but decide to bring two men to your five point. Black rolls 6-4. He decides to move a man from his ten point to his four point and the man on his nine point to his five point. He now has a five-pip lead.

You roll double 2 and use two of the 2's to bring your last two men around the corner to your eleven point and the remaining two 2's to move two men from your eight point to your six point. Black rolls double 4. He brings two men to his six point and two men to his four point. He is now thirteen pips to the good.

You roll 6-3 and bring two men to your five point. Black rolls 5-4 and brings the last man from the ten point to his five point and

Diagram IX-3

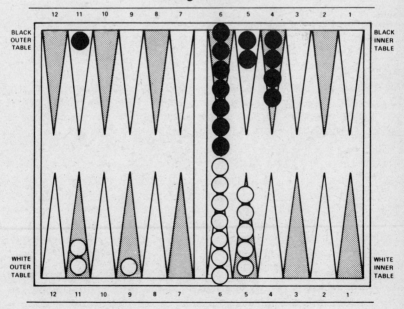

the last man from his eight point to his four point to bring up the
position shown in Diagram IX-3.

You roll 3-2 and bring a man from your eleven point in to your
six point.

Black doubles. What do you do?

If you have been counting along you know that you are eight pips
behind. If you haven't you can check it quickly. Outside your
inner table you are nine pips to the bad. In the inner table you
have three extra men on your five point against Black's four
men on his four point, so you are one pip ahead there for a total
of eight to the bad. Black's pip count is $11 + 48 + 10 + 16 = 85$.

The doubling number (85 divided by 8) is over 10. Black does
have the better of the game but his advantage is not enough to
warrant the double, so you accept.

Black rolls double 5. He moves the man from his eleven point to
his one point and uses the remaining two 5's to bear off the two
men on his five point. You roll 6-5 and bring in your last two men
to your five and four points. Black's lead is up to seventeen pips
and, if he doubled you now (the doubling number is 65 divided
by 17 or less than 4), you would refuse—but he doubled the last
roll and has to play on. You "own the cube"!

He rolls 2-1, the worst possible number. He bears off his man
on the one point and moves a man from his four point to his two
point. You roll 5-3. You bear off a man from your five point and
move a man from your six point to your three point to leave
the position shown in Diagram IX-4.

Black's pip count is now sixty-two and his lead is twelve. If he
were to double you now you would surely take the double in
spite of the fact that the doubling number (62 divided by 12)
is just the least bit over 5. The reason is that Black's position is
so poor. He has no man on any odd-numbered point, hence he
can't bear off a man with a 5, 3, or 1.

This disadvantage becomes apparent when his next roll is another double 5. He brings four men from his six point to his one
point. You roll 6-3 and bear off a man from your six point and
move a man from your five point to your two point. Black's lead
is up to twenty-three pips, but all is not lost for you. He still has
twelve men left on the board.

Black now rolls 4-3 and moves a man from the six point to his
three point with the 3 and bears off a man from the four point
with the 4. See Diagram IX-5.

Diagram IX-4

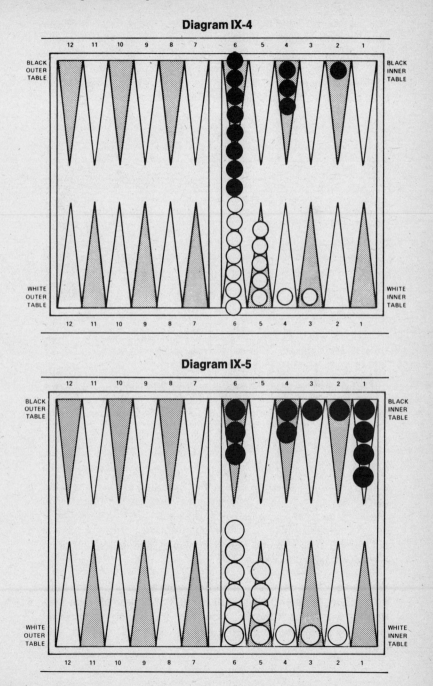

Diagram IX-5

You roll double 3 and bear off two men from your six point. Black rolls 5-2 and can do nothing better than move a man from the six point to the one point and bear off the man from the two point. You roll 5-2 and bear off two men. He rolls another 5-2 and moves a man from his six point to his one point and another from his four to his two point. See Diagram IX-6.

Diagram IX-6

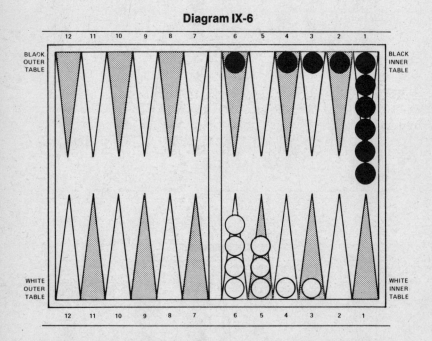

Black's pip count is twenty-one to your forty-six but you are out of the pip count stage now and in the **"counting of rolls to end the game"** stage. You have only nine men left on the board. You can miss once and still get off in five rolls without throwing a doublet. Black is also in a five-roll situation but one miss will put him up to six. You do figure to miss at least twice and don't even consider a double.

You roll 5-1 and bear off a man from your six point. Black rolls 4-1 and bears off two men. You roll 6-3 and bear off two men. He rolls 5-4. He uses the 5 to move his last man on his six point to his one point and bears off the man from his three point with the 4.

Diagram IX-7

Diagram IX-8

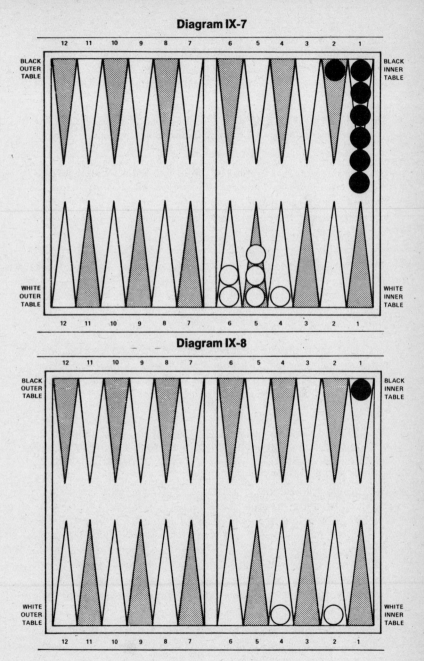

You are now in the position shown in Diagram IX-7 and, if Black doesn't throw a doublet, you have an excellent chance to win. You can miss twice and still get off in four rolls. Your next rolls are 6-3; 4-1; and 6-5. Black rolls 6-4; 5-4; and 6-2. Nice big rolls but 2-1 would have been just as good for him each time.

You are now in the position shown in Diagram IX-8. It is your roll. The cube is on your side and it is clearly to your advantage to turn it to four. (Remember Black doubled to two several rolls back.)

No guarantee goes with this redouble. You have thirteen losing rolls and twenty-three winning rolls. If this position were to occur thirty-six times you would expect to win ten more games than you would lose (23 − 13 = 10) and it is certainly a paying proposition to increase the stake.

Should Black take this redouble? Yes, he should! In those same thirty-six games if he had refused every redouble he would lose 36 × 2 = 72 units. If he took every redouble he would lose 23 × 4 = 92 units and win 13 × 4 = 52 units for a net loss of just 40 units. You don't get rich losing 40 units but you don't go broke quite as fast as when you lose 72 units.

It is also worthy of note to observe that, if Black had waited one more roll before making his unsound double, you would have given up the game and he would be a point to the good instead of sweating out a poor four-point game.

We return now to Game Number 1. In Diagram VIII-2, repeated here as Diagram IX-9, it is Black's roll. He has a three-pip lead, but the doubling cube is on your side. He rolls 5-2 and moves a man from his nine point to his four point with the 5 and a man from his bar point to his five point with the 2, in order to bring men to the open points in his inner table. You roll 6-4 and bring your two men around the corner. He rolls 5-1 and moves a man from his bar point to his two point with the 5 and from his six point to his five point with the 1. He could have brought a man in but decided to improve his board. You roll 6-1 and bring your man on the nine point to the three point with the 6 and a man from your bar point to your six point with the 1. Black rolls 3-2 and brings two men in to his five point to produce the position in Diagram IX-10.

A quick pip count shows that you are still four pips behind, but it is your roll. To all intents and purposes the game is even except that you own the cube.

Diagram IX-9

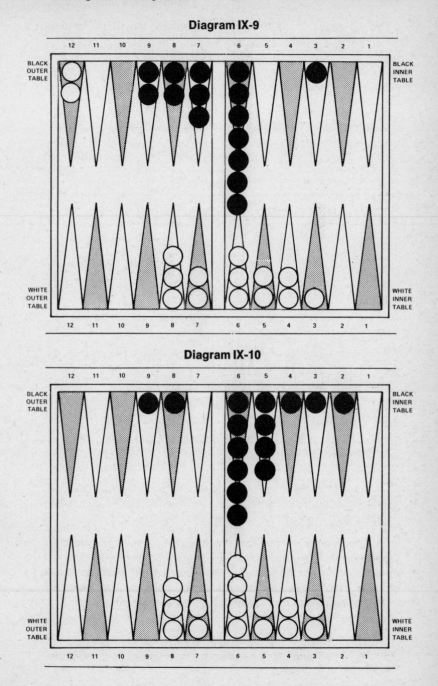

Diagram IX-10

You roll double 4 and bring in the three men on your eight point and one of the men on the bar point. Black rolls 4-2 and brings the man on his nine point to his five point with the 4 and the man on his eight point to his six point with the 2. Your pip count is now 70 and your lead is six pips.

You roll 6-4 and use the 6 to bring the man on your bar point to your one point and the 4 to bear a man off. Black rolls 5-2 and

Diagram IX-11

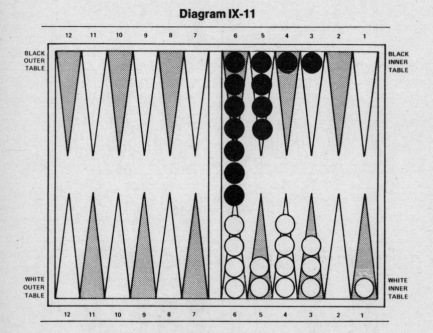

bears off two men to produce the position shown in Diagram IX-11. Your pip count is 60; your lead is nine pips; the doubling number (60 divided by 9) is between 6 and 7.

You should consider a redouble but not offer it because you have fourteen men on the board and your opponent only thirteen. If you never roll a doublet and never miss it will take you seven rolls to get off. If Black never rolls a doublet and never misses it will take him that same seven rolls. Now suppose you each miss once: you will need eight rolls; he will still get off in seven.

Of course, the odds are that you both will miss several times but that little difference is enough so that you should not redouble.

Diagram IX-12

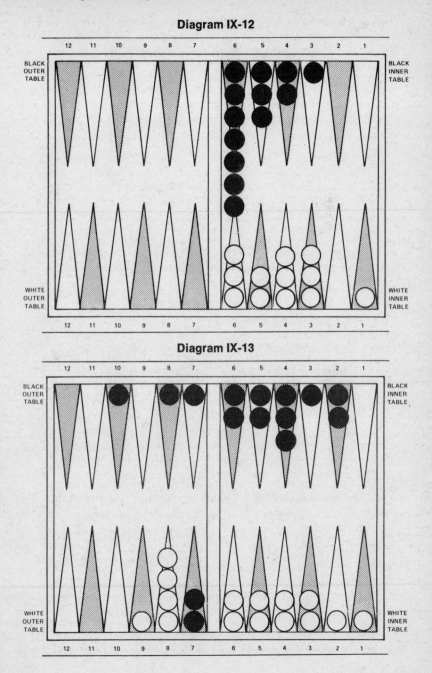

Diagram IX-13

You roll 6-4 and bear off two men. Black rolls 5-2. He makes his best play, which is to use the 5 to bear off a man from the five point and the 2 to move a man from his six point to his four point to produce the position in Diagram IX-12.

Your pip count is 50; your lead is twelve pips; the doubling number (50 divided by 12) is less than 5. In addition each of you is down to twelve men. You should double and Black should refuse the double.

Diagram IX-13 is carried over from Lesson VIII (Game Number 2). Black has just played double 3. Why didn't he do something about his two men on your bar point? Because they represent all the contact left. If your next roll is double 2 or double 6, you will have to leave him a shot right away; in addition, the shot may still come later.

You make a quick pip count to see that yours is 80 and your lead is twenty-two pips. The doubling number (80 divided by 22) is less than 4 and you double.

Should Black accept. No, he shouldn't. There is a chance that he will get a shot but, even if he does get it, he still will have to hit your blot.

Nevertheless, Black does accept and you proceed to roll double 6! You bring the man on your nine point to your three point and three men from your eight point to your two point. Why did you leave the blot on your eight point, rather than on your nine point? It is that matter of giving yourself the best chance to win. The blot on the eight point can be hit by any 1 (11 different rolls). If left on the nine point it can be hit by any 2 and by double 1 (12 different rolls). Remember, when a direct shot is involved, the closer your blot to the threat, the better.

Black rolls 4-2 and moves a man from his bar point to his five point with the 2 and a man from his ten point to his six point with the 4. He does not move the men on your bar point because you just might roll double 1 (after all you did roll double 6 at the wrong time!) and not be able to move that man on your eight point to safety.

Actually you roll 6-2. We won't bother to finish this game. Black might win but he is so far behind that it is pointless for us to play it out.

When to Give and Take End Game Doubles

Diagram IX-8 showed a one-roll position. You were going to win the game or lose it on your next roll since Black was sure to get his last man off if he got a chance to play.

We pointed out that you should double and Black should accept. If your men were on the four and one points instead of on the four and two points, you would have an even stronger double. In fact so strong a double that Black should not accept it. You would win with any one of twenty-nine rolls and lose with only seven (3-2, 3-1, 2-1, and double 1).

If this position were reached thirty-six times and Black took all redoubles he would lose 29 $\times$ 4 (remember you are redoubling from 2 to 4) = 116 units and win just 7 $\times$ 4 = 28 units for a net loss of 88 units. If he refused all thirty-six redoubles he would lose only 72 units.

There must be some point at which it is equally undesirable to refuse or to accept a double. This point is when the doubler's chance of winning is exactly 75% (27 out of 36 in a one-roll position).

Remember this figure. Take end game doubles, no matter how distasteful, if you have better than a 25% chance to pull the game out; refuse them and save money if your chance is less than 25%; let your conscience be your guide when right on the mark.

Counting Rolls instead of Pips

Suppose you and your opponent have six men left apiece and that they are all on the one point. The pip count is even, but you shouldn't bother with it. If no one rolls a doublet, you will be off in three rolls and he will be sitting with two men. If you roll a doublet at either of your first two turns it doesn't matter what he does. You have won. Thus, the only way he can win is for you to roll two ordinary numbers while he rolls a doublet at one of his only two rolls.

If you want exact figures, your chance of winning the game is 1021 divided by 1296, or 78.8%. This is above the 75% mark so you should double and he should refuse to accept your double.

How about eight men against eight men—with all the men on the one point? This is a four-roll position with doublets reducing it to three, or even two.

This position also illustrates the great value of possession of the cube. Suppose you own the cube. If you don't double you have an 88% chance to win the game since at your next turn you will be able to double and end the game unless you roll an ordinary number and your opponent rolls a doublet. In addition, if this last event does happen—and you have retained possession of the cube—you will be able to play the game out to the end and may be able to come back with a doublet of your own.

Now suppose you do double. Your chance to win has gone down to 73% from 88% because your opponent will get to play the game to the end and because if he should get into a redoubling position, you may not be able to finish the game.

Should you redouble in spite of this difference? Yes. Take a hundred games. If you don't redouble, you will win 88 of them and lose 12 for a net gain of 76 units. If you redouble, and your opponent accepts, you will win 73 games and lose 27 for a net gain of 46 games—but the stake will be doubled so your actual gain will be 92 units.

Should your opponent take the redouble? Of course he should. His chance of winning is 27% which is slightly above the 25% mark. He will lose 92 units if he takes a hundred doubles, which is eight units less than the 100 he would lose by refusing.

With ten against ten (all on the one point) you should double, but should not redouble. In other words, you can afford to move the cube from the middle of the table to your opponent's side, but you cannot afford to move it all the way from your side to his. Of course, he should accept.

With twelve against twelve (a six-roll situation) a double is slightly optimistic.

In Diagram IX-14 you are in a six-roll position. Black just might need seven rolls to get off but this chance is not worth considering. What is worth considering is that if Black rolls double 2 or double 3 he will only be able to bear off three men. This will leave him with nine men and he will still need five more regular rolls to get all his men off. In other words, he will not gain anything from a double 2 or from a double 3.

Diagram IX-14

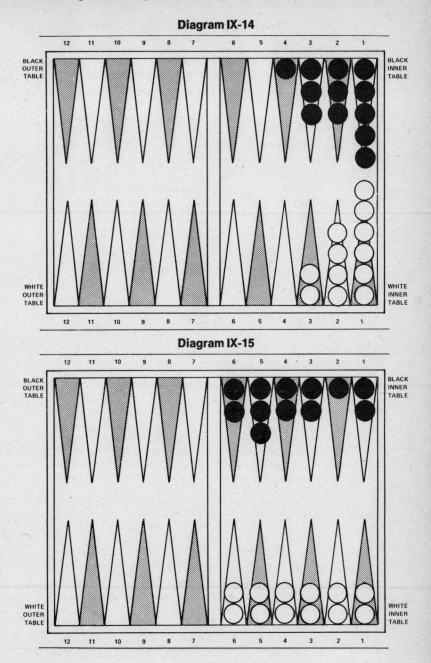

Diagram IX-15

This difference is enough to warrant your offering a first double. It is not enough to warrant offering a redouble.

In Diagram IX-15 you have two men on each of the six points in your inner table; Black has a slightly poorer position since he has three men on his five point and only one man on his two point.

At first glance this looks like a time to count rolls, but it isn't. You are not in a six-, or even a seven-, roll position although you do have a good chance to get off in seven rolls. Instead you should stick with the pip count. Your count is 42 pips; your lead is 3 pips; the doubling number (42 divided by 3) is 14 and your correct procedure is to roll. Do not double at this point.

Lesson X

FINISHING ONE-SIDED GAMES

The position shown in Diagram X-1 is carried over from Game Number 3 in Lesson VIII. The game is one-sided and you are on the wrong end.

You proceed to roll 6-1. You can hit the blot on your twelve point but this would be very bad tactics. Your main interest right now is just to avoid being gammoned. If you hit that blot you will not only be delaying Black's movement of his last men around the board, but you will be creating complications that may result in more of your men being trapped on the black one point or on the bar.

You also don't want to use the 1 to split your men on the one point. If you do split them you give Black a chance to close his board with two of your men on the bar.

Two men back on the one point may get you gammoned—two men on the bar are quite likely to lead to that unpleasant result. So you play a man from your eight point to your two point with the 6 and from your six point to your five point with the 1.

Black rolls 5-4 and moves the men from your bar point to your eleven and twelve points. He doesn't mind leaving a blot because he wants you to hit that blot. You roll 6-3 and bring your men around the corner. Black rolls 6-5 to produce the position in Diagram X-2.

Diagram X-1

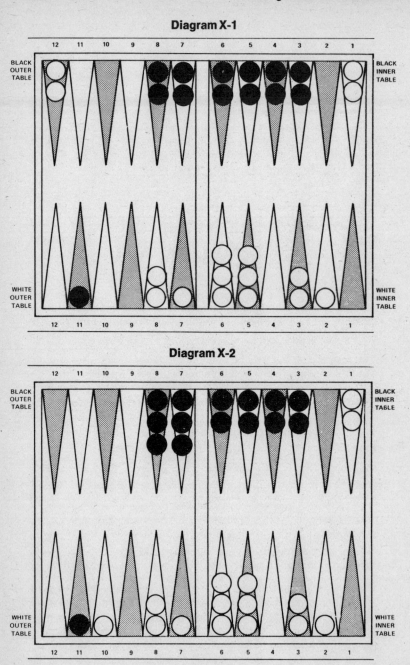

Diagram X-2

You roll another 6-1. The 6 is easy to play. Move the man on your ten point to your four point. You probably start to use the 1 to make your four point but there is a special play for you to make here. Move the man on your bar point to your six point.

You aren't going to get a chance to hurt Black for some time. He may expose a blot on his two point but it won't do you any good to hit it. Eventually he will make his two point and bring all his men into his home table. Then he may give you a shot and, if you hit that blot, you will have a good chance to win the game provided you have been able to retain your six point.

In order to retain your six point you hope you won't have to play damaging high rolls. The highest number you can roll is a 6. Once you get all your men in your home board you just don't have to play that high number at all. Therefore, get your men home right away. The four point will take care of itself later on.

A few more rolls bring you to the position in Diagram X-3. You have managed to hold your board but Black has come in very well and has no immediate bad roll. He does roll 6-1. He bears a man off with the 6 and, if he is an average player, will undoubt-

Diagram X-3

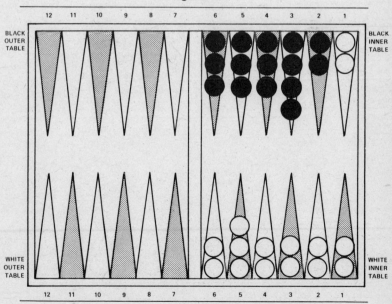

Diagram X-4

Diagram X-5

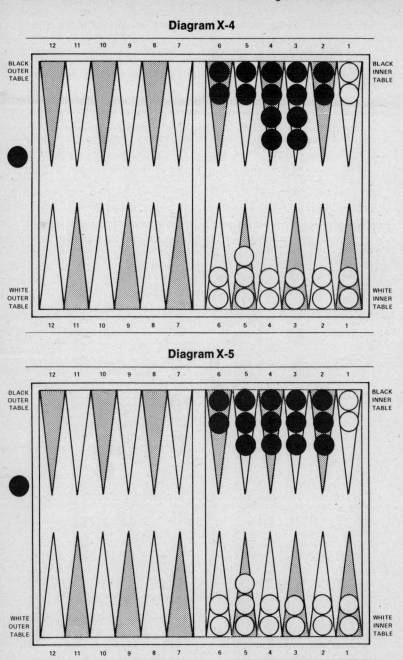

edly use the 1 to move a man from the five point to the four point to produce the position in Diagram X-4.

His reason for this move is that he will be able to play any doublet with complete safety and the average player has learned to guard against positions where the roll of a doublet may force him to expose a blot.

But the expert will move a man from the three point to the two point to produce the position in Diagram X-5 instead. In this position he will have to leave a blot if he throws 6-5, double 6, or double 5, but he will be able to play any of the other thirty-two rolls with complete safety.

Now go back to position X-4. All doublets are safe but one blot must be left with a 5-4 and two blots if the dice show 6-5. There are still thirty-two safe rolls but of the four bad rolls, two will leave two blots.

A player is unhappy when he must leave one blot, but he is miserable when he must leave two!

Diagram X-6 shows the continuation of Game Number 4 in Lesson VIII. Black has just failed to bring either of his two men in

Diagram X-6

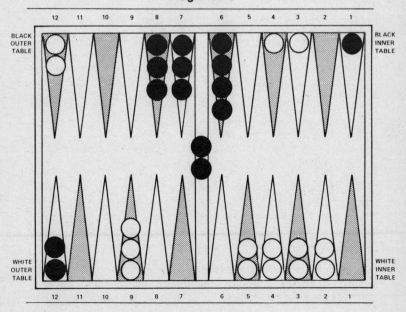

from the bar. You roll 6-2. The six is easy. You cover the blot on your three point. You use the 2 to move the man on the black three point to the five point. The reason for this is to guard against the possibility that you will roll a couple of double 5's and not be able to move that man out of the black inner board.

Black fails to come in. You roll 5-2. Move from the black four to the black nine point with the 5 and from your nine point to your bar point with the 2.

Black rolls 5-1 and brings one man in. You roll double 4. Use three 4's to hit the blot on your one point with a man from the black twelve and the other 4 to move the man on the black five point to the black nine point.

Black fails to come in. You roll 5-4 and move the man on the black twelve point to your four point.

You hope Black won't roll a 6, but the only roll that can really embarrass you is double 6. Actually Black rolls 5-1 and once more brings a man onto the board.

We'll leave the game here. You expect to close your one point and win a gammon. See Diagram X-7.

The Closed Board

When your opponent has one or more men on the bar and you are able to close your board, you are in your best possible situation. You expect to win a game, or possibly a gammon, and the only way you can lose is if you are forced to leave a blot and Black succeeds in hitting it.

There is, however, another danger that many players overlook. It is the danger that you will have to break your board before you can bring your last men into your inner table. Now look at the position in Diagram X-8. You roll 4-1. You use the 4 to close your board. This leaves you three ways to play the 1.

You note quickly that if you use the 1 to move a man from your six point to your five point and then roll double 6 you will have to expose a blot on your six point. You see that if you use it to move either of your outside men you will be able to play double 6 in safety.

If you are careless, you may move your man on the black nine point to the black ten point. You will be safe against double 6, but you proceed to roll double 3. Neither of your outside men

Diagram X-7

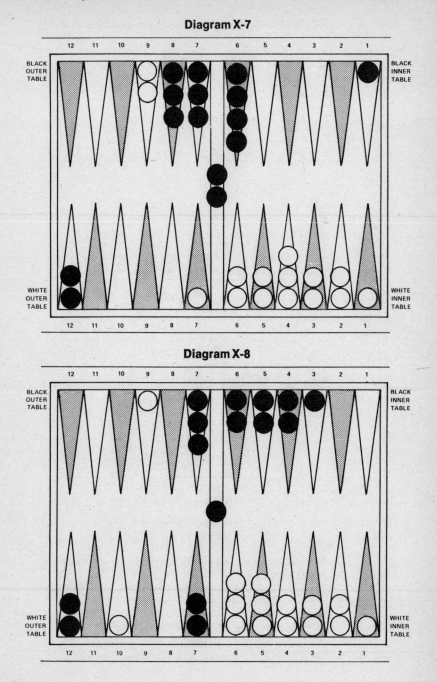

Diagram X-8

will be movable and you will be forced to give up two points in your board.

A careful player will see this possibility and will move his man on his own ten point to his nine point. Double 4 will be a bad roll but he will be able to play it and break only one point in his board. He doesn't want to have to do this but it is better to break only one point than to break two and there is no absolutely safe play.

When in the position of Diagram X-9 you roll 5-1. Your only safe

Diagram X-9

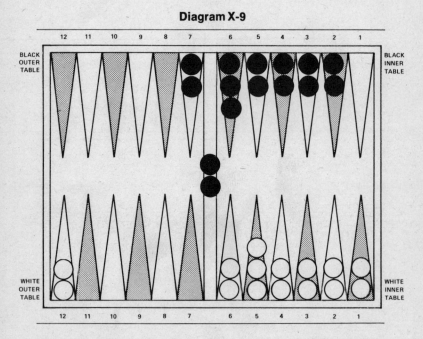

play is to move the two men on your twelve point forward. This will leave you safe irrespective of what your next roll is.

If you play the 5-1 any other way and proceed to roll double 6 you will have to leave a blot.

Get in the habit of being careful with these apparently sure games. With practice you will learn to protect yourself most of the time. There is no such thing as complete protection, how-ever. Thus, you play the 5-1 correctly and follow with 6-4, which you play to the position in Diagram X-10. You are still perfectly

Diagram X-10

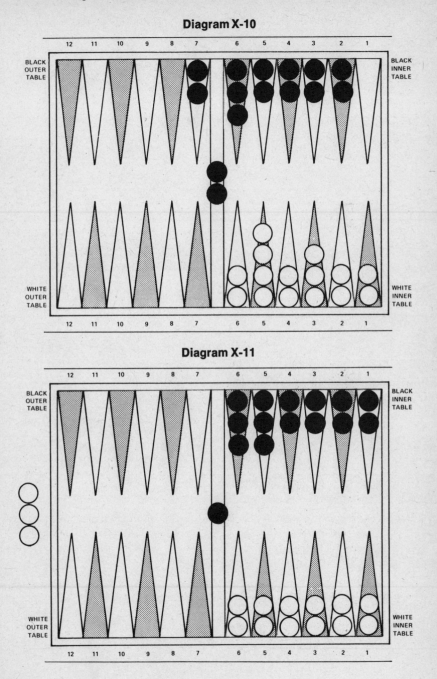

Diagram X-11

Diagram X-12

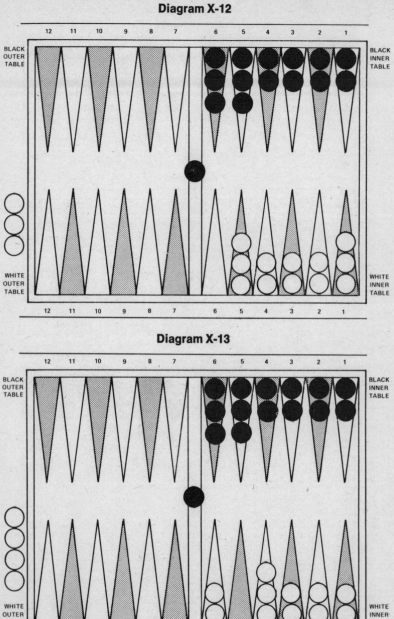

Diagram X-13

safe—but your next roll is 6-1. You must bear off a man with the 6 and move the other man on the six point to your five point with the 1. Now if you follow that roll with double 6, or double 5, you will have to leave a blot.

As you break your board in this and similar positions your game plan should be to break first from the six point, then from the five point, and so on. Diagram X-11 illustrates just about the only exception to this rule. You roll 5-1 and can either break your six point to produce the position in Diagram X-12 or break your five point to produce the position in Diagram X-13.

Let's look at these two positions from the standpoint of your next roll. In either position if you roll double 6, 5, or 4, you must leave a blot. Now look at the ordinary rolls. In position X-12, if you roll 6-5, 6-4, 6-3, 6-2, 5-4, 5-3, or 5-2 (a total of 14 rolls), you will have to leave a blot. In position X-13 the only rolls that force you to leave a blot are 6-1, 5-1, and 4-1.

Thus there are 17 (14 plus the three doubles) blot-leaving rolls in position X-12 and only 9 (6 plus the three doubles) in position X-13.

Diagram X-14

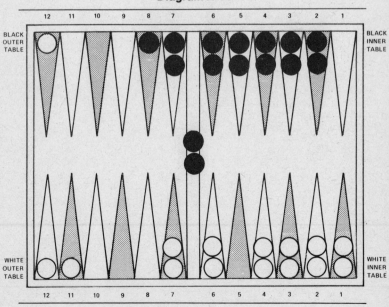

Guarding against a Doublet Rolled by Your Opponent

In the position of Diagram X-14 you roll 4-3. You can move your man on the black twelve point to your ten point and the man on your twelve point to your eight point as your strongest attacking play. This play will leave you with direct shots of 6, 5, 3, and 2, bearing on that open five point. It will also leave you with a headache and a lost game if Black rolls double 5 since with that roll he can bring both men in from the bar and hit your blot on your ten point. Hence, no matter how you finally decide to play that 4-3 don't move a man to your ten point!

Conclusion

When you have an overwhelming position always consider playing for a gammon. When a gammon appears unlikely then play as safe as possible.

Lesson XI

BACK GAMES AND
SPECIAL PROBLEMS

The position in Diagram XI-1 developed after just four plays. You started with 6-4 and ran with a back man. Black's reply was 5-2. He hit your blot with the 2 and moved a man to his eight point with the 5. You rolled 6-5 and used it to bring in your man on the bar and hit his blot on the black eleven point. He rolled 5-1; brought the man on the bar to your five point with the 5 and exposed a blot on his own five point with the 1.

You rolled 5-4, hit the blot on his five point with the 4 and used the 5 to move the man on his eleven point to your nine point. He rolled 4-2, brought the man on the bar in with the 2 and hit the man on your nine point with the 4.

You rolled another 5-4. You made his five point with the 5 and hit his blot with the 4. His fourth roll, 3-2, allowed him to make your two point with the 2 and to move a man from your twelve point to his ten point with the 3.

You should be able to see the reason for all these first plays. He could have used the 3-2 to make your three point; just to bring the man from the bar to your five point; or, instead of exposing a blot with the 3, to move a man from his six point to his three point.

Why did he make the play he did? Because he sees he is well behind and hopes to develop a back game. He has a good start

Diagram XI-1

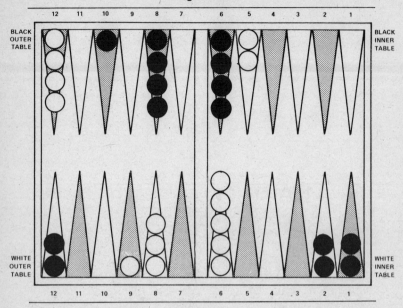

on a back game, but he does not yet have the timing for it. He wants to delay his movement and he offers that blot on your nine point in the hope that you will hit it.

This principle applies in the development of most back games. The man who is behind is not far enough behind to hold a back game. He tries to delay himself by getting you to hit blots. You should do your best not to cooperate. Thus, in this position the last thing you want to do with a 5 is to hit that blot.

If you refuse to delay him in this position Black's best chance is to abandon the back game in favor of a defensive position. To do this he will abandon your one and two points and try to make your four, five, or bar point. He will have the worst of the game but it will be a long time before you become strong enough to double him.

In Diagrams XI-2 and XI-3 you are in the same position against different black back games.

In position XI-2 Black has a really fine back game. He is going to be able to hold points in your inner table for a long time and

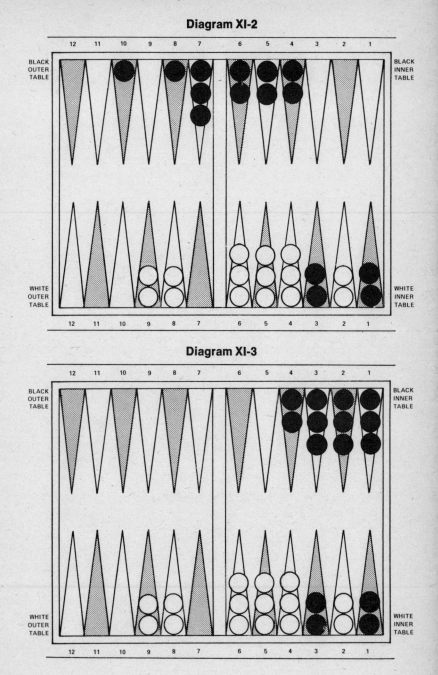

Diagram XI-2

Diagram XI-3

Diagram XI-4

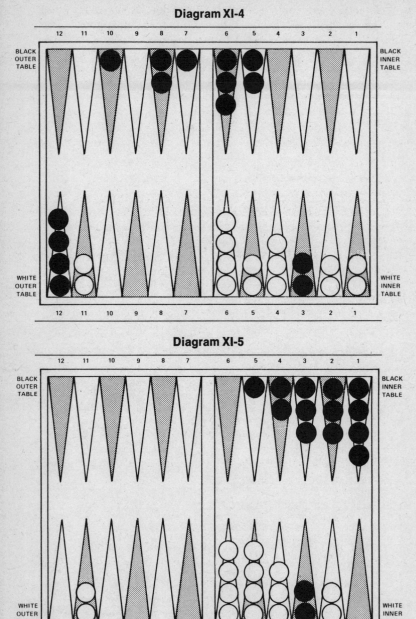

Diagram XI-5

should win the game if he ever hits a blot. On the other hand, if he never hits a blot he will almost surely be gammoned. That is the trouble with back games. If they win, they win; if they lose, they lose double or even triple.

In position XI-3 Black's back game has already collapsed. He has what we like to call a nothing game. Even if you expose a blot and he hits it, you are still a favorite to win.

Therefore, don't go out of your way to develop back games. At best they are a poor gamble.

To Block or Not to Block

In the positions shown in Diagrams XI-4 and XI-5 you have just rolled double 1. You can move the two on your eleven point to your nine point to block a 6 move by either of Black's men on your three point. In position XI-4 that is the last thing you want to do. Black is not going to move those men until he has to. He is far behind in the running game. His one hope is to hit a blot and those are the only men that can do it. If you block his 6's you are also blocking yours. Unless you are lucky enough to roll 5-4, 5-3, 4-3, double 5, 4, 3, 2, or 1, you are going to have to expose a blot to a direct shot.

Leave them where they are or move them forward to your ten point. You still expect to leave a blot but when you do it will be against an indirect shot, not a direct one.

In Diagram XI-5 the reverse holds true. Black wants to move those men if he can. Block off their escape with a 6. You may hold them in chancery until your running game has improved. Furthermore, if one does escape you will be able to hit the other one with any 6, 3, 2, or 1. You may be able to point on him but, even if you can't, hit him!!

Hitting Two Men

Any time you can put two of your opponent's men on the bar he is in trouble. He may get out of it by bringing both men right in but, if you hold just two points in your inner table, he has only sixteen rolls out of thirty-six that will do this for him.

Look at Diagram XI-6. You roll 4-1. You have the better of the game and can play conservatively by moving a man from the black twelve point to your eight point. The trouble with this play is that it does nothing for you. If Black rolls a 4, or double 2, he will make your five point and have an equal game. Other good rolls will allow him to make his bar point or his four point.

Diagram XI-6

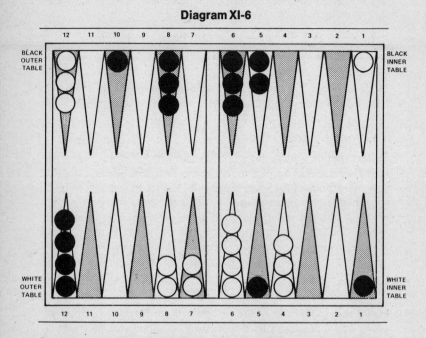

Suppose you hit both his blots with a man from your six point. You might get an unexpected dividend. Black could roll 6-4, double 6, or double 4 and lose his whole turn. If he rolls a 1 his game has improved, but you still have an equal game. If he doesn't roll a 1, or a favorable doublet, you really have done yourself a lot of good.

Attack! Hit the two blots!

In Diagram XI-7 you have a good game and are trying for a gammon. Undoubtedly Black took a bad double some time back and his position has worsened. You roll 6-3. The 6 is forced— you must hit his blot on your one point with it. You can use the 3 to move another man from your bar point to your four point, but this isn't the way to play for a gammon.

Black can roll a 3, or a 2-1, make the three point in your inner table, and practically kill any chance you may have had for a gammon. Or, if he rolls an ace he will hit your blot on your one point and have a good chance to escape from gammon country.

The play for a gammon is to use your 3 to hit his other blot on your three point. This exposes two blots in your inner table but, unless Black rolls 3-1, double 3, or double 1, you should win your gammon.

Hitting a Man to Slow Up Your Opponent

In the position of Diagram XI-8 you roll 4-3. You have to use the 3 to bring your man in from the bar. How do you play the 4?

The safe way is to move the man on your ten point to your six point. This leaves you safe, but probably sorry. If Black rolls any 6, 5, or 3, he can, and almost surely will, hit your man on his three point. Many combinations will allow him to make that point. Other good rolls are so numerous that, if Black were to double you, your only smart course would be to give up.

Suppose you use the 4 to hit his blot on your one point. Your game won't be anything to cause you to burst into cheers, but it will be playable. The chances are that Black won't double; if he does, you can afford to take it.

Diagram XI-7

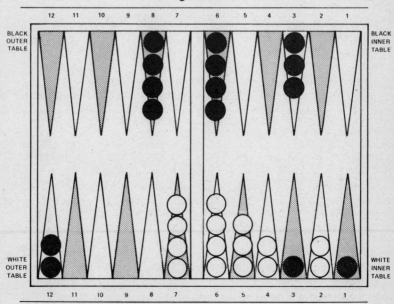

Diagram XI-8

Diagram XI-9

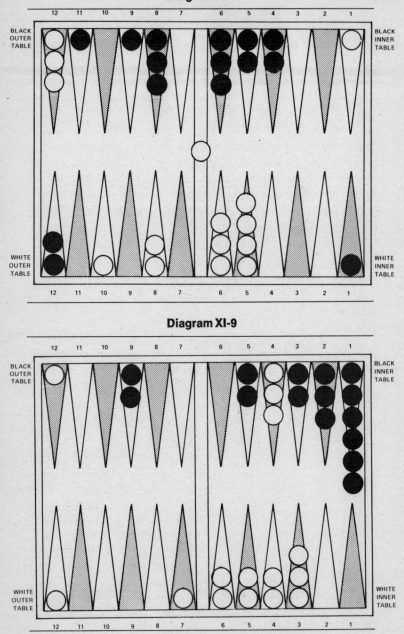

Gambits

In the position of Diagram XI-9 you have some chance to win in a running game. Say one in a thousand. That doesn't mean that your game is hopeless. You have an excellent chance to get a shot and, if you hit, you figure to win easily.

Now you roll 5-2. You use the 5 to make your bar point and your first thought is to use the 2 to bring your man around the corner from the black twelve point.

First thoughts aren't always best and your correct play is to move one of your men on the black four point to the black six point. This play may look silly, but it isn't anything of the kind.

Black can hit that blot effectively with double 3, 5-3, 4-3, and 3-1. In the case of double 3 you are in bad shape regardless of what you have done; in the case of the other rolls he hits you and brings his man to safety. You can hit his blot on the nine point with 6-5, 6-3, or 5-4, but you are unhappy about your gambit.

Now let us look at some of the good things that can happen if you offer up this sacrifice. Suppose Black rolls 6-5, 6-2, 6-1, 5-4, 5-2, or 5-1. That is twelve of his possible thirty-six rolls. He will leave a blot exposed to two direct shots. You will be the favorite to win the game.

Suppose he rolls 6-3. He will hit your blot and be forced to leave that man on his six point exposed to any 6 or to 4-2. How about 3-2? He will probably just give up his five point and hope for a miracle at his next turn.

The other rolls, except for doublets and 6-4, which are good against any play you make, will also be trouble rolls for him. Expose your blot. He won't be happy.

In Diagram XI-10 Black doubled some time back. You took the double because you hoped to get a shot at him but that shot has not materialized. You have just rolled 6-4 and it seems that you will have to give him a shot.

You can move both men forward from the black eight point and only be exposed to any 1 or you can move one man all the way forward to your bar point and leave your blot on the black eight point exposed to 4-1, 3-2, or any 5.

The second play is correct because you don't expect to win this game unless you can send one of his men to the bar. If he hits your blot it is just frosting on the cake for him since all it will do is increase his winning margin.

Diagram XI-10

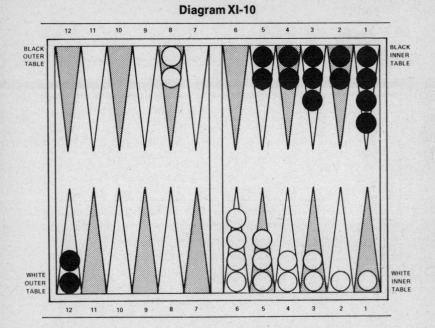

With your man on the black twelve point, if he doesn't hit you with a 1 he goes right by you and wins the running game. With your man on the black eight point if he rolls 6-4, 6-3, 6-2, or 6-1, he has to give you an immediate shot. If he rolls any small number and plays safe by moving forward two of his men in his inner table, you will simply leave your man on his eight point and hope that his next roll will lead to trouble for him.

Diagram XI-11 shows a final gambit. Black was well on his way to gammon you when he had to expose a blot. You hit his blot and this position developed a few moves later. You roll 6-5!

Your correct play is to bear off two men and leave that blot on the six point. If you play safe and he comes right in you have a lost game. If you leave the blot and he hits it you have a chance to hit his man as he continues around the board.

Of course, if he fails to roll a 6 you have an extra man off and, while you aren't the favorite as yet, your position is very good.

Diagram XI-11

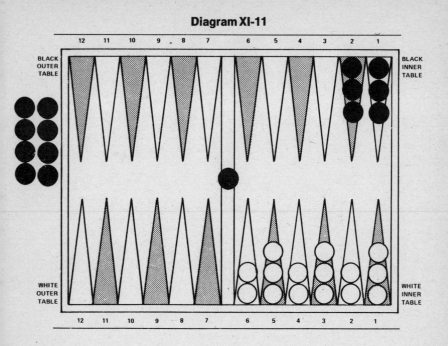

Lesson XII

CHOUETTES AND SETTLEMENTS

When more than two people want to play backgammon, they play what is known as a chouette. In a chouette one man is "in the box," or, more simply, **is** "the box," and plays against all the others.

The man who plays for all the others is known as the captain. He consults with his partners but in the event of argument makes all the decisions except that, when the box doubles, each player has the right to accept or to refuse for himself.

There is a great paradox in a chouette. The box is obviously at a disadvantage. Even the best players in the world make some mistakes and overlook some plays. Several players in consultation are much less likely to do this. In addition, if money is in volved (as there usually is), the box is playing for several times the stake of each opponent.

He may hold back on a double he should give. He may refuse a double he should take. He may take the worst of a settlement of one or all of the games he is playing and, in general, has all the worst of it.

Nevertheless the backgammon player's rationale is such that everyone wants to get into the box. The winner wants to win a lot more, the loser wants to get everything back to get even, and the man who is about even wants the action.

The best chouettes consist of from three to five players. When there are more than five, you have to wait too long after losing to roll the dice again and the money pressure on the man in the box becomes too great.

Now let us look at the mechanics of a four-handed game. The box is playing against a captain and players 1 and 2. If the box wins, player 1 becomes captain, player 2 moves up to number 1, and the ex-captain becomes player number 2.

If the box loses, the captain takes the box, the players move up, and the box becomes player number 2.

If the box doubles, any player who refuses the double loses the pre-double stake and has no further interest in the game. In particular, he is not allowed to give advice about plays or re-doubles. In case the captain is one of those refusing the double the senior player accepting takes over the captain's position for the rest of that game.

If the box loses the new captain takes the box. The other players advance in turn with the ex-captain taking the next to last position in the line and the box taking the last place.

New players entering a chouette start at the bottom of the line in the first game in which they participate.

The captain of a chouette is not obliged to consult with his partners about anything and should not do so on unimportant plays. As an example, suppose he gets first play with a 6 against his opponent's 2. There are three ways to play this first roll. We favor moving a man to your own five point but, if we were playing in a chouette and the captain wanted either to run a man to the black nine point or move one man to the black bar point and another to the white eleven point we wouldn't say a word. The difference between the three plays is not enough to warrant slowing up the game with an argument.

In addition, it is important to remember that there may be times when you have a very strong opinion about a play. If you advise all the time your partners may ignore you; if you just advise occasionally you will be listened to.

When the captain has a real problem with his play, he can ask his partners for advice before moving a man or he can make a tentative move and leave the dice on the table until his partners have a chance to discuss the play with him.

Diagram XII-1 shows such a position. You have doubled the man in the box and he has accepted. You then roll double 4.

Diagram XII-1

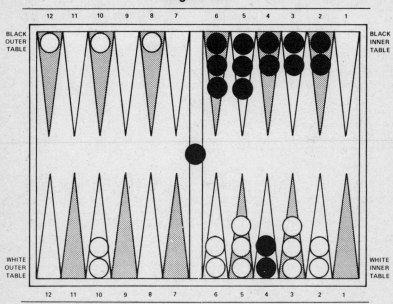

This is a good roll and there are any number of ways to play it. Diagrams XII-2, XII3, and XII4 show the best three of these ways.

XII-2 was produced by moving the man on the black twelve point to your one point and making that point by joining him with one of the men on your five point. This play leaves only one point for Black to enter his man on the bar but, if Black does get that man in quickly, you are likely to have a lot of trouble getting the two men on your ten into your home board without having to leave a direct shot with a 6.

XII-3 results if you use three of your 4's to make your nine point and the fourth one to move the man on the black ten point to your eleven point. It looks good but you are almost surely going to have to give Black a direct 6 or 5 shot later on and may have to leave two direct shots.

XII-4 gets your two men on the ten point into your inner table, makes the black twelve point, and leaves a blot on your eleven point. It has the advantage that you will probably be able to get

Diagram XII-2

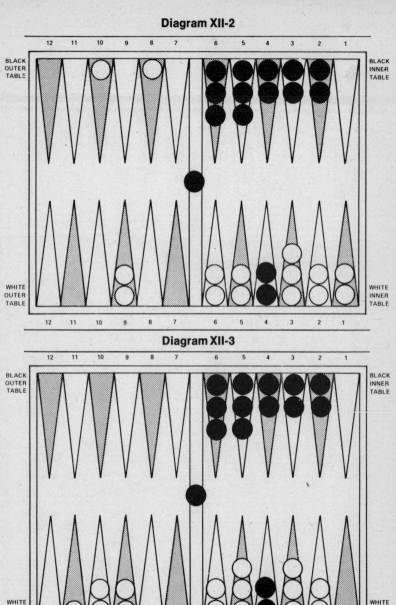

Diagram XII-3

Diagram XII-4

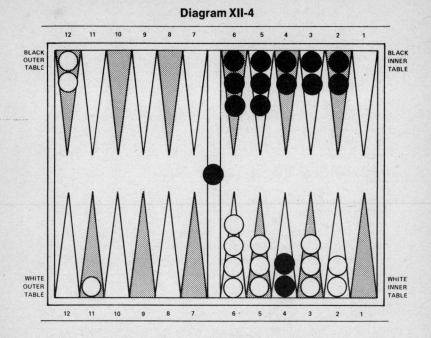

all of your men into your home board without giving any direct shots. It has the weakness that, if you bring in your man from the eleven point and then roll 6-3, you will be forced to use the 6 to move one of your men on the black twelve point to your bar point where it will be exposed to a direct 3. At the same time, your other man back on the black twelve point will be exposed to a 5-4, 6-3, and double 3. The 6-3 and double 3 will hit both of your blots, but the second hit is just another nail in your coffin. The 5-4, however, means that the number of rolls which will cost you the game has risen from eleven to thirteen.

When this situation arose in actual play there were vociferous arguments in favor of each play. The captain finally settled it by moving to position XII-2. Three plays later he had to leave a man exposed on his ten point. Black hit the blot and went on to win the game.

Black might have won the game if White had played either of the other two ways, but no one has been able to convince the other members of the team that the captain had not made a losing decision.

If a player leaves the table during the progress of a game he remains in that game. He may ask some other player to act for him. Otherwise, he acts with the majority of the other players. If he intends to stay away for several games he may ask to continue in the chouette. The other players are not bound by this request and may drop him out at the end of any game. If they let him stay in the chouette he moves up in line steadily to the position of player 1 so that, when he does get back, he will become the next captain.

Deals between Partners and the Box

A chouette represents free enterprise at its best. The partners in a chouette may not agree on their course of action. A player dissatisfied with what his partners are doing may offer to sell his game for a profit, to get out even, or to take a loss. In such case the partner making the deal with him assumes the game that has been given up in addition to his own.

In this and other free enterprise situations remember the maxim, "Let the buyer beware." Don't make deals unless you are sure you know what you are doing.

The box has the right to preempt any deal between partners. Thus suppose the doubling cube is set at 4. The captain offers to give his partners 2 points each for their games and they accept. The box can preempt; pay them the 2 points each and continue just one game.

The box may also initiate and make deals on his own. In this same situation the box may offer 2 points to any man who will take it. Some player may say, "I'll take 3." At this point another player may say, "I'll give you 3." The player accepts his partner's offer whereupon the box may preempt if he wishes.

Of course, the box doesn't always pay. Sometimes he collects. As an example, suppose the box doubles the game from 1 to 2. He rather hopes that some player will give up, but everyone accepts. Now the box is unhappy. He offers to take one-half a point from anyone who will give it to him. Maybe one player accepts, maybe no one accepts, but one man offers to get out even and the box agrees.

When the box offers a deal all of his opponents may accept unless the box makes his offer in some such form as, "I'll take a point from any one player" or some similar offer that precludes settlement by all his opponents.

When the captain settles his game, player 1 takes over. If the captain has settled for a profit he gets to take the box irrespective of who wins the game that is played out. If the captain has settled by paying something he loses all rights and the actual winner becomes the box.

Regular Settlements

A word to the wise here: settlements are for experts. If you get into the habit of settling games you are likely to get all the worst of it unless you know exactly what you are doing.

As an example, look at the position in Diagram XII-5. It is your roll and the cube is at 16. Your chance of winning the game is exactly one-sixth. Your opponent now says, "Your chance is one-sixth. I'll let you out for three-quarters, or 12 points." The offer looks generous but actually is unfair. Let's see what the fair settlement is.

Suppose you reach this position six times. You expect to lose five times and win once for a net loss of four games or 64 points.

Diagram XII-5

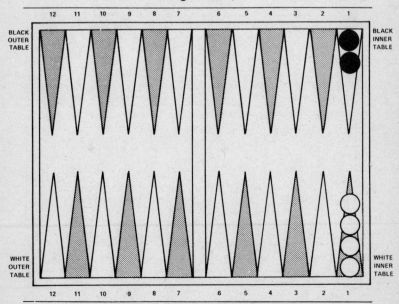

Dividing 64 by 6 gives 10⅔, which is the correct settlement. An offer of 10 would have been generous. The offer of 12 was highway robbery.

Your opponent, however, might have had the best of motives. Most people think that the correct settlement is much larger than it really is and he might have thought that he was being very liberal.

Let's go back to position IX-8. You have just doubled to 4 and your opponent has accepted. Now he offers to pay you one point. How fair is that offer?

In thirty-six games you expect to win 23 and to lose 13 for a net gain of ten games. Your total profit will be 40 units. Divide 40 by 36 and the answer is 1-1/9. He has slightly the best of his offer but it is certainly very close to being correct.

Make your position a trifle better by moving your man from the four point to the three point. Now you have twenty-five winning rolls and expect to show a net profit of 14 × 4 = 56 units in 36 games. Your profit expectation per game has risen to 1-5/9

Diagram XII-6

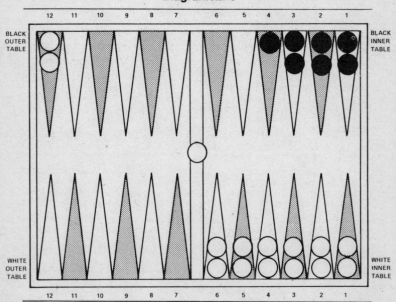

and an offer of 1½ points would be very close to correct. An offer of 2 points would be far too much and 1 point would be far too little.

In the position of Diagram XII-6 it is your roll. If you hit Black's blot as you bring your man in from the bar, you have about an even chance to win the game. If you miss his blot, but come in, the odds are that you will be gammoned. If you miss, but stay on the bar, your opponent will have to leave another blot unless he rolls an ace or double 2. If you miss that next blot, you are almost sure to be gammoned; if you hit it, you still will be unlikely to win the game.

The cube is at 8. What is a fair settlement?

You could work it out by playing a thousand games; otherwise, the best guess is that a fair settlement is that you pay a trifle more than the cube, say 9 or 10 points.

A better way to settle (if all players are in accord) is to play the game (from the present position) four times at 2 points each or twice at 4 points.

You can still win all games and win 8 points or be gammoned every time and lose 16 points. It is likely that you will win one game, lose one game, and be gammoned twice for a net loss of 8.

In making settlements there is no reason why anyone should take the worst of it but, in most of our games, we have a tacit agreement that the man collecting will give his opponent some advantage. Thus, if you are entitled to just over a point and a half, you should be willing to take a point and a half.

Appendix A

PIP COUNT

All else being equal, or nearly equal, the advantage in a running game lies with the player who will require the fewer pips to get his men to his inner table and then bear them off.

Remember that a pip is one of those spots on the dice. When you roll a 6 you advance a man six pips; when you roll an ace you can only advance a man one pip.

Pips don't tell the whole story. At the end of the game, when all of your men are clustered on the one point, a 2-1 roll will be just as good as a 6-5 roll and the mere four pips represented by double 1 can bear off four men for you. However, in the earlier stages of the running game your chance of winning varies directly with the total number of pips it would take you to bring all of your men home and then bear them off.

Experience can give you a rough idea of how you stand but, just as radar is better than a seaman's eye, so an accurate pip count is better than a backgammon player's judgment.

It is very little trouble to learn to count pips. It will slow the game a trifle, but you don't need to make a pip count at every turn to play. Thus, in the early game you have a rough idea as to who has the better of any potential running game. If you have been rolling higher dice and none of your blots have been hit, you will clearly be in front; if the reverse is true, you will be behind.

When behind you try to complicate the position; when ahead

you try to simplify it so as to get into a running game as soon as possible.

Now let's get around to an actual pip count. The count for men in your inner table is easy. It is 6 for a man on the six point; 5 for a man on the five point; and so on. It is just about as easy for men in your outer table. A man on the bar point has a count of 7; a man on the twelve point, a count of 12; other men, counts of 8 to 11 according to the point which they occupy. It is harder to make a count on your opponent's side of the table. For one reason, the numbers are larger; for another, you just can't use the number of the point they are on.

There are all sorts of mathematical formulae for counting these pips but we don't use any of them. Instead we know that the pip count for a man on the enemy twelve point is 13. For any other man in his outer table we count 13 plus the number of pips necessary to bring him to that twelve point. Thus, a man on the black bar point counts $13 + 5 = 18$.

For men in the black inner table we know that a man on the five point counts 20. Men on lower-number points count 20 plus the distance to the five point. In the rare event we have a man on the black six point we note that it is one less pip than a man on the five point, or 19.

At the start of the game your position is even. Let's see what your pip count is. The two men on the black one point count 24 each (total 48). The five men on the black twelve point count 13 each (total 65). The three on your eight point count 8 each (total 24) and the five on your six point count 6 each (total 30). Thus your count is $48 + 65 + 24 + 30 = 167$.

Let us now look again at Diagram II-3, reproduced as Diagram A-1. You will recall that we used this position to illustrate the use of the simplified method of counting combined with the backgammon player's eye. Your exact count is 39 (for the three men on the black twelve point) $+$ 32 (for the four men on your own eight point) $+$ 30 (for the eight men in your inner table) $=$ 101. Black's exact count is 36 (for the two men he has on your bar point) $+$ 22 (for the two men he has on his own eleven point) $+$ 52 (for the eleven men he has in his inner table) $=$ 110.

Note the increased accuracy of this method of determining your position relative to that of your opponent. The simplified count showed that he had the best of it. The simplified count combined

Diagram A-1

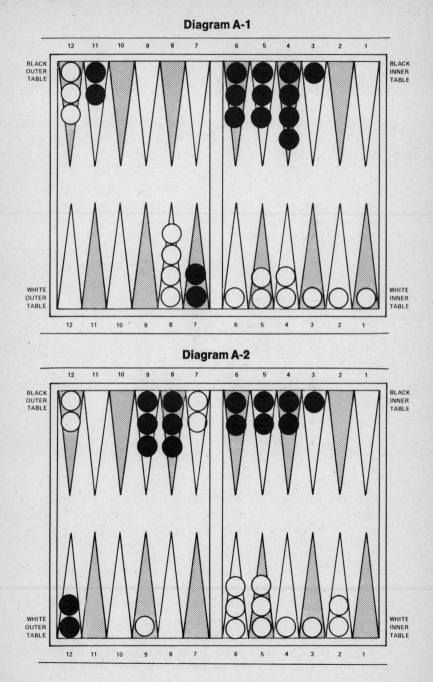

Diagram A-2

with the backgammon player's eye showed that you had a possible edge. The exact count showed that you were nine pips—over one roll—ahead!!

If you just want to know your relative standing it is always possible to just count the net differences. In the position in Diagram A-2 you haven't bothered with a pip count because neither you nor Black has been considering the idea of doubling since your men on the black bar point and his men on your twelve point are likely to have a lot of trouble passing one another.

Then you roll double 3. You want to move your men forward from the black bar point if you will be in good running shape; you want to keep them back there if you will be behind. You move tentatively to the position in Diagram A-3 and make a quick count of the net differences between your pip count and Black's.

Diagram A-3

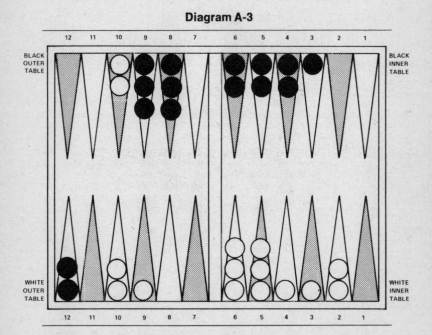

Your two men on the black ten point need two pips each to balance the two black men on your twelve point. You are four pips behind. You charge yourself another two pips to bring your two men on your ten point forward to your nine point where you will then have three men to balance Black's three men on his nine point. You are now six pips behind but you gain 24 to go 18

ahead when you count Black's three men on his eight point
against him.

Thus you are 18 pips ahead before starting to count the men in
the inner table. You lose 6 for your extra man on the six point
and 5 more for your extra man on your five point to cut your
lead down to 7 pips. His extra man on his four point exactly
balances the two men you have on your own two point.

Since you will be 7 pips ahead after you play, you change your
tentative move to an actual one by picking up the dice.

If you want to keep a running score of the net difference as play
continues, you can do so. Thus Black rolls 6-1. He was 7 behind;
he is now even. You roll 6-3 to go 9 ahead; he rolls 5-2. You are
still 2 pips ahead and it is your roll. Not enough to consider
doubling.

If you feel that making a pip count is too much trouble, and that
you can't add very well anyway, remember you really don't need
complete accuracy. If you miss by a pip or two it isn't going
to have any great effect on your decisions about running, doubling, et cetera. You still will be doing better than if you just look
the position over and try to guess how you stand.

Diagram A-4

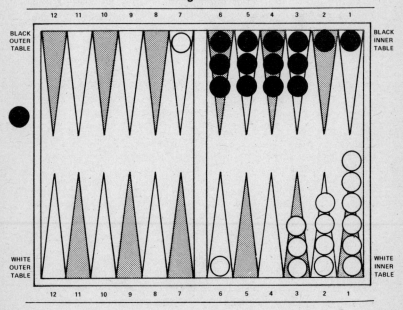

On the other hand, if you learn to make completely accurate pip counts, don't get too fond of your nice toy. Study your position for effectiveness. In general, if several of your men are clustered on one or two points while your opponent's (with the same pip count) are spread around, you have the worst of the position; if your men are spread more than his, you have the better of it.

The position in Diagram A-4 developed because Black had two of your men caught on his one point by a prime. While he was bringing his remaining men around the board you were forced to keep moving men forward in your inner table. Eventually he broke his prime and you immediately rolled double 6 to bring one man to the black bar point and one man to your own six point. He rolled 5-1, bore off a man from his five point with the 5, and moved a man from his two point to his one point with the 1.

It is your roll. Your pip count is 47. Black's pip count is 57. Your lead is 10 pips and the doubling number (see page 91) is less than 5. From a pip count alone your position is so good that you should redouble and he should refuse. From the standpoint of practical backgammon this pip count means nothing. It will probably take you two rolls to get your man on the black bar point around to your inner table. It may even take more. Meanwhile, he will have borne off several men. You may win the game, but right now he is still the decided favorite.

Appendix B

THE OFFICIAL LAWS OF BACKGAMMON

In 1931 Wheaton Vaughan, the Chairman of the Card and Back-gammon Committee of the Racquet and Tennis Club of New York, invited representatives of other clubs to join with the Racquet Club in producing a Code of Laws for Backgammon. The code was prepared and accepted. Oswald Jacoby is the only member of the original committee still alive.

The laws to be presented here, which conform closely to the old ones, were prepared by Jacoby and John Crawford, in conjunction with the Inter-Club League of New York and the International Backgammon Association, and, as far as we know, appear in all modern books on the game.

The laws should never be used to gain an advantage over your opponent. They are designed to prevent arguments, not to cause them.

The Game

1. The game of backgammon is played by two persons.
2. Thirty men, fifteen of one color and fifteen of another, are set up as shown in Diagram B-1 on a standard board of four quarters or tables having six points each.

   In Diagram B-1 the players' home boards (or inner tables) are

Diagram B-1

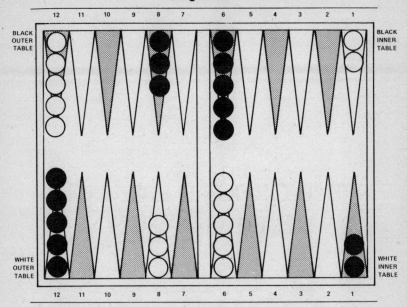

shown at the right. This means that White's home board is opposite his right hand, and Black's home board opposite his left hand. In actual play it is customary to have the home boards nearer the light.

3. For entering and bearing off, the points in both inner tables are considered as numbered from one to six, beginning with the point nearest the edge of the board.

4. Direction of play is from the adversary's inner table to the adversary's outer table, to player's outer table, and then to player's inner (home) table.

5. Play of the men is governed by two dice, thrown (cast) from a cup in which the dice are shaken before casting.

6. (a) For the first game either player may ask to roll for choice of seats, men, or dice. Otherwise they just sit down, set the men up, and play.

    (b) At the start of any later game either player may ask to mix the dice. In this case he shakes the four dice together in one cup and rolls them out. The opponent selects a die

—then the roller—then the opponent—with the roller then taking the last one.

The Throws

7. For the opening throw, each player throws a single die. Each tie requires another opening throw. Whoever throws the higher number wins, and for his first move plays the numbers upon both dice. After that each player in turn throws two dice.

8. The dice must be shaken thoroughly, rolled together, and come to rest flat (not "cocked") upon the table at the player's right, otherwise they must be thrown again.

9. There must be a rethrow if a throw is made before an adversary's play is completed.

10. A play is deemed completed when a player moves his men and starts to pick up his dice. If he starts to pick them up before playing all numbers he legally can, his opponent has the right to compel him to complete or not to complete his play. A roll by the opponent is an acceptance of the play as made (see Law 19).

The Play

11. The play of the men consists of:
    (a) Moving a man (or men) the exact number of points indicated by the number on each of the two dice thrown. One man may be moved the total of the two dice thrown, or one man may be moved the number shown on one die, and an entirely different man the number shown on the other die.
    (b) Entering a man, in the adversary's inner table, on a point corresponding to the number on a die thrown.
    (c) Bearing off a man in the player's inner table, when no man is left outside that table or on the bar, in accordance with Law 17.

12. Doublets require four plays of the number on the dice.

13. Plays must be made for both dice if possible. Either number

may be played first. If either number may be played, but not
both, then the higher number thrown must be played.

14. No play may be made which lands, or touches down, on a
    point held by two or more of the adversary's men.

15. When a play lands on a point occupied by a single man (blot)
    of the adversary's, such a man is "hit" and must be lifted from
    the board by the hitter and placed on the bar in the center of
    the playing board, to await entry in accordance with Law 11(b).

16. A player having a man on the bar may not play any other man
    until that man has been entered.

17. When in position to bear off, you may bear off a man from a
    point corresponding to the number on a die thrown, or from
    the highest occupied point which is lower than the number
    indicated by a die. If the number is thrown for an unoccupied
    point, no man below can be borne off, using such number,
    while any man remains on a higher point. You are not required
    to bear off a man if you are able to move forward on the board.
    Law 13 applies here as in all other situations.

    For example, in Diagram B-2 you roll 6-1. You may use the
    1 to move from your six point to your five point, and then use
    the 6 to bear a man from the five point; thus, you don't leave a
    man exposed to a hit by Black's men on your one point. In
    other words, Law 13, stating that *as long as you play both
    numbers you may play either one first,* applies in bearing off
    as well as at all other times.

Errors

18. If an error has been made in the set-up, it must be corrected
    if either player notices it before the second play of a game has
    been completed.

19. If an error in play has been made, either player may require
    its correction before a subsequent throw, but not thereafter.
    The man played in error must be correctly played if possible.

Scoring

20. A game is won by the player who first bears off all of his men.
    A gammon (double game) is won if the adversary has not
    borne off a single man. This doubles the count.

Diagram B-2

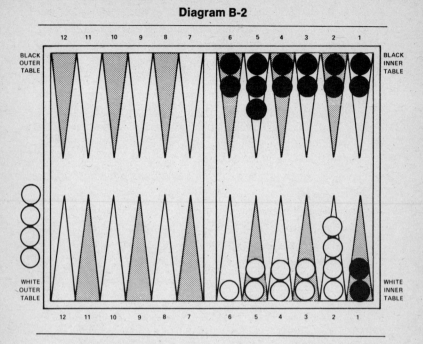

A backgammon (triple game) is won if the adversary has not borne off a single man and has one or more men in the winner's inner table or upon the bar. This triples the count.

21. Doubling game. The count is raised:

(a) *Automatically:* Each tie in the opening throw doubles the previous count. Automatic doubles are not played unless the players have agreed to use them and an understanding has been reached as to the method and limitations of such doubles.

(b) *Voluntarily:* Either player may offer the first optional double of the previous count. After that the right to double the previous count alternates, being always with the player who accepted the last double.

A double or redouble may be offered only when it is the player's turn to play and before he has thrown the dice. He shall be deemed to have thrown the dice even if he rolls cocked dice.

A double may be accepted or declined. The refusal of a

double terminates the game, and the player refusing loses whatever the count may amount to before the double was offered.

22. Gammons double or triple the last count.

Chouette*

23. Chouette is played by three or more members.
24. In beginning the game each member shall throw a die. The one throwing the highest number is then the "man in the box," the next highest is the "captain." The other members, in accordance with each one's throw, rank below the captain and succeed him in that order.
25. The initial throw shall determine each member's position, but in the event of a tie only those tying throw again for their position. The highest or higher number always has precedence.
26. Any applicant to a chouette may be accepted. He becomes the last ranking member in the first game in which he participates.
27. After the positions have been determined, the man in the box and the captain proceed as in the two-handed game except that all the remaining members are partners of the captain.
28. The man in the box plays alone and scores separately against each one of his adversaries. He retains his position until defeated. In such event, he retires as a player and takes his place as the last ranking member (unless there be an added member). The previous captain then becomes the man in the box.
29. The captain may consult with any or all of the partners on any question that may arise in the course of the game. He is, however, the final arbiter, except as hereafter provided. Should he be defeated, he loses his position and takes his place as last ranking member (unless there be an added member). The highest ranking partner then becomes captain.
30. All partners are bound by the action of the captain except in

*In a chouette too much discussion and contention slows up the game. The captain should ask for advice only when he is really in doubt as to the play, and partners should give advice only when they think the captain is overlooking a play entirely or when they want to suggest that he double.

the case of a double by the man in the box. In this case any player has the right to refuse or accept the double, irrespective of the action by the captain.

31. Should the captain decline to accept a double offered by the man in the box, he loses his position and forfeits to the man in the box his count previous to the proposed double.

32. When a double has been declined by the captain, any or all of the other members may accept it. The highest ranking of those accepting becomes captain until the termination of that game.

33. Accepting or declining a double does not change the rank of any member when the new captain loses; if the new captain wins, he takes the box.

34. Those players who refuse to accept the double are out of the game and may not consult from then on.

Postscripts to the Laws

Learn the Laws of Backgammon and follow them. Making your own laws leads to anarchy and can ruin an otherwise fine game. Still there are some modifications that you may want to play. We will start with something for chouettes.

Modification for Chouettes

In some chouettes the captain may arbitrarily insist on doubling a game even though his partners don't want to. According to the Laws the captain's decision holds, but most players prefer:

(a) When the captain insists on doubling and *a majority of his partners object,* they may demand that the captain pay them off at the current game stake. In this case the man in the box has the right to preempt and pay them off.

(b) When the captain insists on doubling and *half or less than half of his partners* object, the objectors may withdraw from the game entirely. In this case the man in the box has the right to demand that the captain take over their games.

This rule has one very salutary effect. It keeps the captain from making silly doubles and redoubles.

Modification Pertaining to Undoubled Games

This is sometimes called the Jacoby Rule because Oswald Jacoby was the first person to have suggested it. It provides that, unless a double has been made and accepted, either player can concede a single game at any time.

Sometimes a player gains an overwhelming advantage right at the start. He may decide to play on for gammon, rather than double and end the game immediately. This leads to a long, boring game.

The Jacoby Rule should not be played in tournaments, or matches, but it is fair to all players and makes regular backgammon more fun.

Optional Rerolls

Some people go double crazy. They like to see the cube at 32, 64, or even higher. In order to get there they allow several automatic doubles at the start of the game. Some of these come from optional doubles. You roll 2 and your opponent 1. You refuse this roll, turn the cube to 2, and roll two dice. If your reroll happens to be a doublet you turn the cube to 4 and play the doublet.

Now your opponent makes his first play. If he doesn't like his roll he turns the cube up a notch and rolls again. If he gets a doublet either time, that also moves the cube up.

Initial Double Dice

Double dice lead to even more automatic doubles. In this game each player rolls both dice initially. High man plays first (doublets count as plain total only; double 3 is just six).

If the high man does not like his roll he has the option of turning the cube and rolling again. The second player also may reroll if he wishes to do so.

A doublet turns the cube; if each player rolls the same total the cube is turned. If they roll identical rolls it results in two turns of the cube. Suppose each player starts by rolling double 4. This turns the cube right to 16. Two doubles for identical rolls and one double for each doublet.

When you play this type of game for any stakes at all you should put some limitations on the cube. One way is to determine an upper and a lower limit. The best ones are 4 and 8 (or 8 and 16). Then remember if you start all games at 4 or 8 you are playing for a stake which is, at the least, four times the agreed amount. A dollar a point becomes at least a four-dollar game.

As for playing without limitations, just refuse to. If you play for just a nickel a point and let the cube start at 1024 you are playing for over fifty dollars a point, which is a far cry from a nickel.

Technique of Double Dice Play

The only technique of double dice play is to remember you don't have to reroll. If you start with 3-1 or 6-1, take your roll. On the other hand, if your opponent starts with double 1, which puts the cube at 4, don't reroll to get it to 8. Take your beating at 4.

GLOSSARY

Around the corner.   When you move a man from the opponent's side of the board to your own side you are said to be moving him around the corner.

Automatic doubles.   A modification of the normal rules, automatically doubling the stakes at the beginning of a game if both players roll the same number in tossing for first play.

Back game.   Defensive strategy employed by a player when his position is such that he sees no chance to win a running game.

Backgammon.   If, when you bear off your last man and thus win the game, your opponent not only has not borne off a single man but has one or more men in your inner table or on the bar, you have won a backgammon, and the stake, if any, is tripled.

Back men.   Men in your opponent's inner table. You start the game with two back men on your opponent's one point.

Bar.   The strip in the middle of the board which separates the inner and outer tables, usually raised.

Bar point.   Each player's seven point.

Bearing off.   Removing your men from the board, in accordance with the Laws, after you have moved all fifteen of your men into your inner table.

Block.   *See* Making a point.

Blocking game. A defensive game where you try to impede your opponent's progress by placing blocks, or made points, in his way.

Blot. An "exposed man," *i.e.* a single man on a point.

Board. Either the entire backgammon table or one of its four parts—synonymous with "table."

Box. The "man in the box" in a chouette. He plays against all other players in the game.

Break a prime. *See* Prime.

Builder. A blot which is in good position to help make a point or a third man on a point.

Captain. In a chouette, the leader of those playing against the box.

Chouette. A form of backgammon for more than two players.

Closed board. When you have made all six points in your inner table you are said to have a closed board.

Cocked dice. Dice which do not come to rest flat upon the board.

Combination shot. *See* Indirect shot.

Come in or on. To bring a man from the bar into your opponent's inner table. Also called "entering," "reentering," or "entering from the bar."

Contact. Positions where all of one player's men have not yet passed all of the opponent's men; positions where theoretically it is still possible for one player to hit the other's blot.

Counters. *See* Men.

Count the position. *See* Pip count.

Cover a blot. Move a second man to the point occupied by your blot and thus make that point.

Cube. *See* Doubling cube.

Cup (or dice cup). The cup in which the dice are shaken before being cast.

Dice, die. Plural and singular for the cubes used in casting. They are normal dice with each of the six sides being marked with one to six dots, or pips.

Direct shot.   A position where the blot is 6 or less points away from the opponent's threatening man; one where the blot can be hit if the proper number appears upon either die. *See* Indirect shot.

Double.   To offer to increase the game stake by doubling it. If the opponent declines the double the game is over.

Double game.   Same as a gammon.

Doubles or doublets.   The same number is thrown on both dice. When you roll a doublet you must play that number four times.

Doubling cube.   Sometimes merely called the cube. An over-sized die with the six faces marked with the numbers 2, 4, 8, 16, 32, and 64. It is used to keep track of the number of units for which the players are playing at any stage in the game. When a double is offered and accepted the cube is turned to the next higher number.

Early game.   As the name implies, the first part of the game.

End game.   The last stages of play. The tactics employed by the players toward the end of the game.

Enter.   *See* Come in.

Exposed man.   *See* Blot.

Gammon.   If, when you bear off your last man and thus win the game, your opponent has not borne off a single man you have won a gammon and the stake, if any, is doubled.

Hit.   Moving one of your own men to a point occupied by one of the opponent's blots. You are said to have hit that blot. The blot, after being hit, is picked up and placed upon the bar.

Home board.   *See* Inner table.

Indirect shot.   A position where the blot is 7 or more points away from the opponent's threatening man; one where it takes a combination of both numbers on the dice for the blot to be hit.

In the box.   In chouette the box (or man in the box).

Inner table.   The quarter of the board comprising the first six points. Men are entered or borne off this table. Same as inner board, home table, or home board.

Lead.   The difference in the pip count of the two players.

Lover's leap.   The move of one of your back men from the oppo-

nent's one point to the opponent's twelve point when you have
thrown a 6-5.

Making a point.   You are said to have made any point which
you occupy with two or more of your men; your opponent's men
cannot touch down or land on such a point.

Man in the box.   *See* Box.

Men.   The counters, discs, or checkers, which you move around
the board during the course of play. A player has fifteen men of
the same color. His opponent has fifteen men of a different color.

Off the board.   When a blot is hit it is sent off the board.

Outer table.   The quarter of the board comprising points seven
to twelve. Same as outer board.

Pip.   One of the spots on the dice.

Pip count.   The number of pips needed to bear off all of your
men (assuming no waste motion). Same as counting your position.

Point.   Each of the twenty-four narrow triangles on the board,
twelve on each player's side.

Point on a blot.   To hit a blot at the same time that you make
the point it had occupied.

Position.   The location of your men and your opponent's men
at any given time in the game.

Prime.   Six consecutive made points anywhere on the board.
Your opponent cannot move a man past your prime. When you
remove all (or all but one) of your men from one of the points
forming the prime you are said to break your prime.

Rail.   Same as bar.

Redouble.   Offering to double the game stake after a double
has been previously made. It can only be offered by the player
who accepted the last double. It can, of course, be refused or
accepted. If refused the game is over.

Re-enter.   *See* Come in.

Running game.   The position in which all of each player's men
have either passed or are nearly certain of passing all of his
opponent's men.

Safe, or safety.   Moving a second man to a point occupied by your blot. Same as cover a blot.

Semi-back game.   A player who is behind holds his opponent's four or five point and tries to impede his progress while at the same time running with his other men.

Set up.   The original arrangement of the men on the board. See Diagram B-1 in Appendix B on the Laws.

Staying back.   Keeping some men in your opponent's inner table as part of a back game or a semi-back game.

Table.   Same as board. Usually used, however, in connection with the qualifying terms "inner" and "outer."

Taking off.   Same as bearing off.

Triple game.   Same as backgammon.

Ⓟ

Quality Non-Fiction for Every Interest—from PLUME Books